Only a Gringo Would Die for an Anteater

Only a Gringo Would Die for an Anteater

by

MICHAEL H. MILTS, D.V.M.

with

CARL LARSEN

McGraw-Hill Book Company

New York   St. Louis   San Francisco   Bogotá   Guatemala
Hamburg   Lisbon   Madrid   Mexico   Montreal   Panama
Paris   San Juan   São Paulo   Tokyo   Toronto

1 2 3 4 5 6 7 8 9 0   FGFG   8 6 5 4 3 2 1 0

Reprinted by arrangement with
W. W. Norton & Company

First McGraw-Hill Paperback edition, 1980

Library of Congress Cataloging in Publication Data

Milts, Michael H
  Only a gringo would die for an anteater.

  Reprint of the ed. published by Norton, New York.
    1. Milts, Michael H.   2. Veterinarians—New York
(City)—Biography. I. Larsen, Carl
joint author. II. Title.
[SF613.M54A36   1980]   636.089′092′4 [B]   80-36674
ISBN 0-07-042391-1 (pbk.)

Contents

Only a Gringo
Would Die
for an
Anteater

1
Raunchy

Raunchy was usually as playful and friendly as your average three-hundred-pound housecat. Somehow, the majesty and dignity we associate with his species was missing from his personality. He was just too lovable to be a lion.

He had been treated with care and affection since first coming to the Central Park Zoo, a stunted little creature with poor bone shape and a skin condition resembling mange. I had worked hard on him, and our friendship grew. Eventually, he paid me the ultimate compliment. He let me put my arm in his mouth. So when I made my regular Wednesday visit that November afternoon, he was glad to see me.

With a flick of his paw, Raunchy sent his favorite toy,

a bowling ball, crashing against the bars of his cage. He was obviously in the mood for a game of catch. But he was in for a surprise. As the Chief Veterinarian for the New York City Zoos, I had treated animals of about every size, shape, and appetite, but this was the first time I'd ever been called upon to perform a vasectomy on a lion.

Some form of birth control was definitely in order. The rough-and-tumble antics between Raunchy and his cage-mate, Sapphire, were beginning to look suspiciously romantic. He was nearing his third birthday and about ready to discover the birds and the beasts. Unfortunately for Raunchy, big cat cubs are a glut on the market. They are being exterminated in the wild because their habitats are being destroyed, but in zoos they breed so well that no one needs the babies anymore. And if we let Raunchy and Sapphire follow the sometimes rocky but inevitable course of nature, the cubs could easily wind up in the hands of a government-licensed dealer and eventually be sold to a shooting preserve. There are a number of laws protecting spotted cats in America, but none for lions.

A castration would have been simpler, but the side effects are undesirable. A castrated lion often loses his regal mane, his physical fitness, and what might be called his lust for life. We didn't want Raunchy to develop an inferiority complex, so vasectomy seemed to be the answer.

I started talking to Raunchy as I took off my coat. Cheerful, friendly, nonsense talk. I think a positive cage-side manner is as important for a vet as the well-known bedside manner is for an M.D. Most animals can sense friendship in you as easily as they sense uncertainty or fear. If you spend half your life dealing with animals the size of mobile homes, you've got to exude self-confidence. The trick is being able to draw the line between being fearless and being foolhardy.

A uniformed parks attendant came into the building, looking puzzled.

"Doc," he said, "your car stinks."

Dr. Rochelle Woods, the young vet who worked with me at the time, covered her mouth and giggled.

"My car doesn't stink," I said, "it's a Rolls-Royce." Indeed, it was. Maybe a trifle under the weather, but still a Rolls. And just because we had loaded the trunk up with baby skunks the day before and driven them out to a New Jersey animal farm was no reason to put it down.

"Well, I'll just . . . open it up, and air it out a bit. And keep an eye on it," he said and left.

Dr. Woods was suddenly very busy and avoided my withering glance.

As I was filling a hypodermic with tranquilizer, antispasmatic, and antisalivant, Raunchy came up to the front of his cage to watch. I stopped to rub his ears. A real pussycat. His foot-long tongue, lolling in ecstasy, brushed like sandpaper across my arm.

"Good boy, Raunchy," I said, "everything's gonna be okay."

Gray-clad parks employees began drifting into the building to help with the operation. Several of them carried snatch poles: long aluminum poles with adjustable rope loops at the ends, for handling large animals. The building, which houses both primates and cats, was closed off to the public.

The Central Park Zoo has an outstanding collection of baboons, chimpanzees, and gorillas—including Pattycake, one of the first gorillas born in captivity. They all must have sensed that something was up as soon as the door closed. Their immediate chorus of high-pitched screeches alerted the cats, and the hollow room echoed with animal warning sounds.

They distracted the lion, and he began to pace nervously. The attendants shooed Sapphire through a gate and into an adjoining empty cage. She left with little complaint. Sapphire is nearly as friendly as Raunchy and often nudges him aside when recognized humans show up. Still, she manages to maintain the sultry aura of the ageless female.

Sapphire is approximately the same age as Raunchy, but there is no way to tell exactly. She had been sitting in the window of a Fifth Avenue apartment one day when a startled neighbor spotted her and called the A.S.P.C.A. They deemed such a report worthy of investigation and checked it out. Sapphire's owner calmly explained that he had bought her for a few dollars, raised her from a baby, and was in the process of finding a larger apartment. The truth of the ancient saying had become clear to him: As your lion grows, so shrinks your living room.

Manhattan landlords are notoriously cool to pets of any kind. And smuggling a lioness into your abode, hidden under your raincoat, takes a tenant of rare size and aplomb. So with a mixture of reluctance and relief, the owner turned Sapphire over to the Society for the Prevention of Cruelty to Animals. They didn't know what to do with her either. She ended up as a gift to the

Central Park Zoo, much to the growing delight of Raunchy.

I inserted the drug-laden hypodermic into a specially designed pistol while Dr. Woods was filling a second. The din from the other animals lessened a bit, and Raunchy quieted down. I wanted to make the first shot a good one. When you are shooting a friend, the second shot always seems to hurt both of you. I took a bead on his flank and pulled the trigger.

The noise sent the primates into a frenzy. The high-pitched popping sound, magnified in the spacious room, became quite loud.

Raunchy whirled as it hit him, his beautiful light brown eyes settling instantly on me. Accusingly, I thought. Then he commenced to race about the cage, his growls approaching a roar. Zoo lions aren't much good at roaring. Perhaps having regular meals served up on a platter has something to do with that. But Raunchy came close.

The apes howled and skittered about until they were assured that none of their tribe had been injured, then they settled down to offer criticism of the rest of my afternoon's work.

The lion blossomed in his anger. His favorite toy caromed around the cage like a pinball. He shook the hypodermic dart from his skin almost immediately, so we couldn't know how much of the fluid had gotten into his system. Judging by his activity during the next few minutes, it was very little. Raunchy was bent on taking the zoo apart, brick by brick.

"Not much of a shot," I said.

Rochelle nodded. The tranquilizers we had used, 20

ccs of ketimine and 4 ccs of Ace promazine, must have failed to penetrate. We set up another charge.

As Raunchy loped to the back of his cage and turned, I hit him slightly behind the foreleg, in the thinner skin around the ribs. He twisted, trying to get at the second dart with his teeth, but it was solidly implanted. The report from the gun sent the other animals into a symphony of shrieks that must have shaken the chandeliers at Tiffany's.

Raunchy was both angry and frightened. I apologized under my breath as a trickle of blood stained his ribcage. Anesthetizing a large animal is not as simple as it looks on television.

He circled the cage constantly, his breath becoming more and more erratic, and his long, graceful bounds shorter. Finally he stumbled, sat back on his haunches, and keeled over.

I hurried to the stock room to scrub up in the sink. Any operation on a tranquilized animal the size of Raunchy is an iffy thing. Speed is essential, for your own life and limb as well as that of the patient. It only takes one eyeball-to-eyeball meeting with an awakening grizzly bear to convince you of that.

Dr. Woods and I climbed into the cage, along with four parks attendants carrying snatch poles. Together, we rolled Raunchy over onto his back and applied an eye ointment. It would protect his corneas from injury if he failed to blink under sedation. I injected another 30 ccs of tranquilizer, while Rochelle administered antibiotics.

The sounds of the nearby carousel drifted in: strange background music for an operating room. The light was poor, and the floor of Raunchy's cage would have to serve as a surgical area. The Bronx Zoo is a private business and has a large staff of vets, but the city-run zoos—Central Park, Flushing, and Prospect Park—have little in the way of funds or equipment. We have to make do on a limited budget.

Spread-eagled by the ropes on his legs, Raunchy still twitched in his sleep. The operation, performed before an audience of skyscrapers and apes, took nearly an hour. Shortly after I'd made the first incision, my eyes began to fill with tears.

Dr. Woods passed me a towel and I mopped my face. "What's wrong?" asked one of the attendants.

I sniffed, wiped the tears from my puffy eyes, and admitted the truth. "I'm allergic to cats," I said.

Dr. Woods wrapped the surgical tray while I washed up. The operation looked good, but I was hoping Raunchy would feel under the weather for awhile—long enough for it to start healing. The tubes that I had severed and tied off had been located quite deep in the lower abdomen, and Raunchy would need several days rest. We left him sleeping peacefully under the watchful eyes of half a dozen attendants. Among the parks employees, he was easily the most popular character in the zoo.

We walked through the thinning crowds toward the maintenance building. Children still broke away from their parents and raced excitedly from cage to cage. Man's fascination for other forms of life has never slackened, and for me it's become a life-long odyssey. When I was a child in Queens, it wasn't quite the closely packed borough of New York City that it is now. There were dairies within biking distance of our house, and I spent many hours observing the placid animals in pasture. I can't remember ever wanting to be anything other than a veterinarian. When my application was accepted at Cornell, one of the leading veterinary colleges in the United States, it seemed to me only the natural progression of things.

At the zoo office, I phoned Flushing, the open-air animal park near Shea Stadium. Things were quiet, they said; no real need for me to drive out. I was always available for an emergency at any of the City zoos, of course, and could occasionally skip a routine Wednesday visit. I began to think of taking at least part of the afternoon off. I needed time to pack.

I've always been drawn to the wilderness areas of the world and have visited many of them. They are a strange mixture of beauty, peace, and danger, and usually provide a test for one's self-reliance. The excitement of such a challenge had been growing in me for several weeks, as I'd been invited to join an ecological expedition into the Amazon jungle. Due to the pressure of work, I had put off assembling my gear and taking care of the thousand details that living in an urban civilization made necessary. It was to be an extended trip, and I'd obviously need more than a toothbrush and a change of socks.

"How are things at Prospect?" asked Dr. Woods as she came into the parks office.

"I'm calling them now," I said. "Nothing doing at Flushing."

She was eager to get on to Prospect Park and check out the new arrival. The day before, a polar bear cub had been born there and was being bottle-fed and watched around the clock. Polar cubs are incredibly small at birth, when you consider the size of the mothers—usually around eight inches long and weighing less than a pound. Sheep dog puppies are the same size, and they never get bigger than a hundred pounds, while adult polars can reach 1,200 pounds.

This one had been lucky to survive the first moments of birth; its mother had a habit of eating her newborn. It was rescued by a sharp-eyed attendant who managed to distract the mother and, using a rake, rolled the cub near enough to grab up unharmed.

There seems to be no logical pattern of behavior in animals when it comes to cannibalism. If it's done in the wild, no trace is left. And in captivity, it seems to be more a matter of whim or individual temperament than anything else. So we have tragically learned that, even within the same species, you just can't tell about mothers.

At the other end of this behavior spectrum, there is a black bear cub in the Flushing zoo that has two mothers—a nearly unheard-of family pattern, especially among bears. The two mothers delivered young at about the same time. One of the cubs died and for reasons completely unknown the mothers are sharing the survivor. They both suckle it, tutor it, and treat it as a natural child. From what we know of bears in the wild, this could just never happen. The real mother would attack any living thing that got near her cub. Any other bear, male or female, would give ground immediately.

I had driven out to see the polar cub shortly after it was born. It looked healthy, and we had hopes that it would live, separated from the mother. The mortality rate is high in the Arctic; the climate is harsh and food is scarce. But in our more temperate zone, there are equal dangers. A cub is subjected to a whole universe of bacteria that it wouldn't have encountered in the North.

I hung up the phone. "The cub died."

Rochelle busied herself packing up our equipment, and said nothing. It was a lousy way for us to get off work early.

The aroma of yesterday's skunks lingered in the car as we drove back to my office. We were both silent, trying not to feel the loss of the polar cub. The treatment of animals is a lot more than a business, and maintaining a strictly professional attitude at all times is impossible. Losing a member of an endangered species only makes failure worse.

We pulled into the garage a block from my office and started to unload. "I'm getting a new car," I said, more to break the silence than anything else. "This one stinks."

2

The Menagerie

Murray Hill is a slight bump on the mideastern side of Manhattan Island where narrow office buildings, brownstones, and fast-food joints stand shoulder to shoulder. There are probably more animals in the area now than when it was bought from the Indians by Peter Minuit for sixty guilders. It's a good location for a veterinarian, if you like unusual clients who tend to keep rather odd pets.

I opened a street-level office there, just around the corner from Lexington Avenue, in 1966, and live in an adjacent brownstone.

There has been some controversy among the vet trainees who study with us, as to who runs the place. Opinion is split about evenly. Some think the practice is a well-oiled machine, moving like clockwork despite a strange array of egotistical office pets. Others leave with the impression that the staff and I are actually bullied into competence by the animals that have taken up permanent residence. Both sides of the argument probably contain some truth, but all agree: it's a menagerie.

The small waiting room is full of plants, vivariums, and cages for homeless or abandoned animals. We have been able to find homes for several hundred pets a year from among our clients and their friends.

Most of our clients are truly concerned humans, and once in a while we witness a real Cinderella story. Two elderly ladies found a very gentle tomcat who had evidently been in one fight too many. They picked him up in the street and brought him in to be euthanized, which means administering a concentrated dose of anesthetic. It is a painless process and the animal goes to sleep before death occurs.

The jet-black tom had a terribly infected eye, almost totally destroyed, but we thought he could be saved. I had to enucleate the eye, but with sufficient care it healed. We vaccinated him and put him up for adoption in one of the waiting room cages.

Other animals arrived, were treated, and found owners. This one stayed. No one wanted a one-eyed cat. It was a shame, because even though he'd grown up in the streets, he was quite gentle. We began to think of him as a permanent fixture.

One day a client brought in his dog for shots and his best friend for company. The friend was well dressed and distinguished looking. And he was wearing an eyepatch.

The man and the cat spotted each other immediately, and a silence seemed to descend on an office normally filled with honks, hoots, and hisses. He walked over to pet the cat and was met with a large, rattling purr.

"Obviously," he said to the cat, "we were made for each other."

He turned to Caroline, the receptionist who had been with us for about a month, and quite formally said, "I'd like to adopt this animal."

She smiled, nodded vigorously, and sniffled loudly.

Being near living and growing things has always made me more comfortable, an attitude I inherited naturally from my father. As the tract homes and housing complexes blossomed around us in the borough of Queens, we had to roam farther and farther afield on our Sunday afternoon hikes. We explored much of Long Island—which had a surprising variety of wildlife—together.

Scarlet fever left me physically depleted and badly stuttering as a child. My father gently guided the interests of a shy and self-conscious boy into a concern for the world of nature. A gradually increasing program of physical activity restored my health. The natural extension of that program—competitive sports—gave me the confidence I needed to overcome the stuttering. My father was certainly not displeased when I decided to go into veterinary medicine.

My grades at Cornell were good, but not spectacular. The pre-med and pre-vet courses were identical, and I had to work at it. Oddly enough, the requirements for entering their graduate veterinary school were higher than those for the graduate medical college.

I boxed as a welterweight—short, wiry, maybe even a bit cocky, but convinced that I couldn't lose. Fighting, for one reason or another, has been part of my life for as long as I can remember. Twice, due to broken vertabrae in my back, I've been told I would never walk again. Being stubborn is sometimes a virtue.

After college, I answered an ad in a veterinary journal. Sidney Kessler, a D.V.M. in Brooklyn, had an opening for an assistant. Our friendship started the moment I walked in for the interview, and I stayed for five years, learning the profession under his good-natured direction. Then, under bare lightbulbs and in hock for the equipment, I opened an office in the Murray Hill section of Manhattan.

Clients trickled in. Enough, bringing dogs and cats, to keep things running and pay the salaries of a secretary and Bill Webster, my assistant. I made house calls and fancied myself a sort of urban country doctor. It was a lovely fantasy, but no more than that. Within a few weeks, I learned why Dr. Kessler—except in cases of extreme emergency—stuck to "Office Hours Only."

An artist called one afternoon with two problems: she had a sick dog and very little money. Would I, she wondered, accept some of her paintings in exchange for treating the animal? Our office walls were starkly bare at the time. I agreed to make a house call that evening.

After we closed the office at six o'clock, I took my bag, drove downtown, and located the building. The artist lived in a giant fifth-floor loft, surrounded by condemned buildings and vacant lots. My knock was answered by what sounded like a thousand dogs, barking and scrambling to get to the door.

The artist opened the door and peered out into the dim hallway, holding back a full platoon of dogs and angry, trampled cats. All breeds, all colors, all sizes, and all excited.

"You the vet?" she asked.

"That's right," I said, clearing my throat and preparing to run. She looked much too frail to stem the tide of attacking animals. She turned, shouting and kicking at them, then beckoned me in.

The smell of unwashed animals was overpowering. My eyes began to water, due to my allergy. I wiped them and looked around. I had never seen walls or floors quite that color before. It looked as though she had covered them with burlap that moved in a slight breeze. Except there was no breeze. Her impressionistic paintings, stacked everywhere, gave off the same weird, three-dimensional effect—caused, I assumed, by my own free-flowing tear ducts.

"Here's the sick one," the woman said, moving toward one of the dogs. The floor seemed to crackle under her feet.

I followed her, moving slowly to assure her animals I meant no harm. As I neared the wall, I realized that it wasn't covered with burlap at all. It was covered with ticks—millions and millions of them, crawling up and down over each others' bodies.

Carefully I knelt down and examined the sick dog. His friends watched me closely throughout the diagnosis. Satisfied, I stood up, wrote out a prescription, and gave the artist directions for administering the medicine.

She nodded and waved casually at her paintings.

"Help yourself," she said, "I really appreciate this."

I selected two small paintings and shook the parasites off of them. "You've got ticks," I said.

"Yes, I know. They're hard to get rid of. I step on them whenever I can." She opened the door for me. "I don't use insecticides," she smiled. "They upset the balance of nature."

I left. Her dog recovered, and she comes into the office from time to time with another sick pet. Despite the balance of nature, her pets get thoroughly sprayed before being examined.

During the past dozen years, a cast of thousands has passed through our office, and a few of the most tenacious have stayed on. The only pet I ever actually bought was Barnaby, our resident movie star. He shared the camera (if not the billing) with Al Pacino in *Serpico* and was the veteran of a hatful of television commercials. I think he wanted to play character roles but was always, unfortunately, typecast as a sheep dog. The other members of the menagerie, like Clarence, started out as walk-ons.

Clarence had cauliflower ears and massive scar tissue around his eyes. He was the sorriest specimen of cat I'd ever seen. Brought in for disposal, Clarence responded to handling like he'd just heard the bell for round one. The fact that he was three-quarters dead didn't dampen his spirits; he was determined to go out scratching and biting.

But I recognized a kindred soul. *Mike,* I said to myself, *this cat has been through it. This is the cat you've been looking for.* I decided to try to save the gray and white splotched bundle of multiple injuries. Two operations and extensive treatment followed, despite his clawing protests while going under anesthetic.

We kept him caged for nearly a month, as he recovered. During that time, he gradually quit attacking everything in sight. But he stayed wary.

I took him upstairs and turned him loose on my apartment. That first evening Clarence killed three mice I didn't know I had, then virtually disappeared for three months. Once in awhile I'd open a cabinet and find him curled up there, but I'd never find him in the same place twice. I didn't push him, figuring he had as much right to privacy as anyone else.

Then one day I was sitting in an easy chair reading, and he came out, hopped up next to me, and that was it. The delicate compromise that cats eventually make with these bothersome humans had been reached. We're friends, separate and individual, and he's taken on several self-appointed duties to pay his keep. If someone is at the door—even if it's Barnaby, scratching irritably to survey part of his kingdom—Clarence, with all the gruff courtesy of an ex-boxer, lumbers over to answer it. I may not need an official bouncer at the door of my apartment, but you can never tell.

Clarence never comes down to the office. It seems to be a territorial agreement he has worked out with a gaunt yellow creature named Stanley. I'm not sure whether Stanley has a respiratory ailment or a psychiatric problem. His growl is like the mating call of a trash compactor, and his gentlest purr reminds one of a handful of ball bearings dropped carelessly into a blender. He is totally self-sufficient. When he's thirsty, he paws at a faucet until it's turned on. When he's hungry, he eats whatever is at hand. Among the office cats, he's top dog. But like all heads of state from Hamlet to Hitler, he has a fatal flaw.

His arrival at the office was a violent one. A girl walked in and unceremoniously proclaimed, "My husband and I are breaking up, and I don't need *this* anymore!" *This* was a kitten, which she bounced off our fish tank, then turned and walked out. So much for introductions.

Our receptionist picked the cat up and it immediately started to purr. "I think it's got something stuck in its throat," she said. Even as a kitten, Stanley's voice was unusual. We were hoping his voice would change when he reached puberty. It did. For the worse.

We found Stanley a home with a man from the neighborhood. But after he had put out a kitty pan, some food and water, and had gone out for an hour, Stanley trashed his apartment. The drapes came down, the furniture was shredded, lamps and china were broken, and the walls were autographed. The man brought him back. Stanley purred.

An elderly couple took him in. He ate a mattress and a couch one night, while they were out. We couldn't understand it; when he was returned, he hung around the office people and was as pleasant as the first day of spring.

His third owner had to check into a hotel until he could rebuild his house.

Stanley's psychological kink finally dawned on us. He needed company, constantly. We gave up trying to farm him out and kept him at the office. From time to time, he'll still get shut into an examination room by mistake and will go berserk. Otherwise, he's cheerful and gregarious and greets patients and owners with his friendly, grinding purr.

The only time I can recall him ever being happily left alone was the night he got locked into a closet with a twenty-five pound sack of cat food. Bill Webster came in early the next morning to feed the animals, opened the closet, and a round yellow thing rolled out. A closer inspection revealed it to be Stanley, bloated beyond belief. His eyes were glazed in the aftermath of an eating orgy. He couldn't quite get his legs under him, but he kept trying to roll over for a last clawful from the nearly empty bag. Who says there's no Cat Heaven?

The staff and I more or less work around him, though we are under his constant scrutiny. The other cats—Gloria, Chip-Chip, and Arnold (who is completely blind, but knows the office as well as your tongue knows the inside of your mouth)—all defer to Stanley. Some of them have been declawed and some haven't. It has no effect on where they stand in the pecking order.

A lot of mistaken humanitarians seem to think that declawing a cat is like cutting off the fingers. Nothing could be farther from the truth. If a frisky cat is clawing up the furniture and threatening domestic tranquility, I usually recommend declawing. Most of the time just the front claws are trimmed, and a cat can certainly catch mice just as well using his teeth and back claws. It's a lot better than turning him out in the streets, where his life expectancy is less than a year.

There are many stories about that tough old alleycat

who hangs around a neighborhood for years and is recognized by everyone. The grim truth is that the various humane organizations in the New York area have to euthanize a thousand animals a day, and few street cats survive a winter without help.

A tarantula and a scorpion live in adjacent vivariums on a shelf over my bed. Certainly not what one would call house pets, but observing their behavior patterns has become a hobby that fascinates me. My friends thought I was a bit crazy when I began to take an interest in more dangerous and exotic animals. Perhaps, in my work, I have overcompensated for being prone to injury. But there are all kinds of crazy. I think that people who smoke in bed, for instance, are a lot crazier than I am.

Having a sense of humor, as well as a sense of humanity, is essential in this profession. But back in the first bleak days when we opened the office, it was hard to keep our spirits afloat when it looked like the ship was sinking. Our first brush with what we thought would be a truly exotic animal turned out to be an amusing case of mistaken identity.

It was a relatively busy day, for a newly established vet. I had administered two distemper shots, performed a minor surgery, and there were still three clients in the waiting room.

I walked up the narrow hallway that separates our examination and surgery rooms from reception and told Sharon, our first secretary, that I was free.

"Mike," she asked, "do you treat birds?"

"Sure, why not? They taught me birds at school." I

smiled at the assembled clients. They had brought two dogs and a nervous cat in a cardboard box. Not a bird in the crowd.

Sharon returned to the phone, assured someone that we do, indeed, treat birds, and hung up. She looked up at me and said, "Know anything about condors?"

There was a momentary silence before I said, "Well, yeah. They're giant vultures. They've got the biggest wingspan of any bird in North America. Something like sixteen feet."

"Then they may have a little trouble getting it through the doorway."

"Someone's bringing in a condor?" asked one of the dog owners.

Sharon nodded.

I treated all three animals during the next hour, but their owners sat in the waiting room chatting, awaiting the arrival of the big bird.

A well-dressed couple walked in, and Sharon asked for their name.

"Schwinn," the man said.

"Schwinn? You called about the condor?"

He nodded, and set a box on her desk. A very small box. He opened it and a multicolored bird about the size of a sparrow cocked its head and looked up at us.

"That's not a condor," I said.

"I know," said Mr. Schwinn, "it's a conure. A conure parrot. You treat parrots, don't you?"

The clients who had waited all stood up, glanced at the tiny bird, and left. It was my first exotic animal. Ron and June Schwinn, a couple I came to know and respect, had quite a menagerie of their own. It included Indian leopard cats, a kinkajou, and a coatimundi that they had to donate to a zoo because it kept picking the lock on its cage and intimidating their dogs.

Rather hastily, I took the conure into the examination room. Despite its size, the conure parrot is a vile-tempered and individualistic creature, and I was sorry I hadn't donned the heavy leather gloves we had ready to handle a condor.

It had a cold. I treated it with antibiotics and returned it to the Schwinns. They had no trouble getting it out the front door.

When Dr. Woods and I returned from Central Park, Caroline, our secretary, was on the phone. She saw us, looked relieved, and covered the mouthpiece. "You've got a call," she said.

"Out to lunch," I said. The loss of the polar bear cub was still on my mind and I was in no mood for a personal call.

"This lady says she has to talk to you." There was a grim note in Caroline's voice.

I took the phone. "Dr. Milts. Can I help you?"

"I want to have my cats destroyed."

I recognized the voice. The lady had two beautiful Persian cats that had been in for shots and regular check-ups. They were well fed, pampered, and, last time I'd seen them, two of the most contented felines in Manhattan.

"What seems to be wrong?" I asked.

"There's nothing wrong with them," she said, a trace of impatience in her voice, "I just need them destroyed."

I asked her why.

"I've had my apartment redecorated, and the cats don't go with the furniture."

She must have mistaken my silence for an inborn interest in the skill of her interior decorator, because she launched into a description of her new suede-and-leather living room.

Finally, I interrupted. "Don't you think you could find a home for them?"

At least she was honest. "I can't be bothered," she said, "just kill them. I can afford it."

"How about if I could find someone to take them off your hands? They're beautiful cats, should be no problem. Would you bring them in?"

It was her turn to pause. Although sounding slightly annoyed, she agreed to bring them in and hung up.

Dr. Woods saw the expression on my face. "What's wrong, Mike?" she asked.

"Oh. We lost a customer."

"Scary, right?" said Caroline as I handed her the phone. She was right. The sad thing is, it wasn't the first time we had encountered that sort of attitude. The owner of a pair of registered two-year-old collies had come in several years before and insisted that we euthanize them. She was being moved to another city by the company she worked for and was unable to take the dogs along.

The woman was absolutely positive that the animals —in a very literal sense—couldn't live without her, and no amount of arguing would change her mind. Shortly after that incident, we set up cages in the waiting room to help find homes for other such victims of whim.

We had no trouble, of course, placing the two Persians. Their new owner was delighted, even though they didn't match her decor.

The next morning we got an emergency call from Central Park. Raunchy had ripped out his stitches and was bleeding badly. I grabbed a clean surgical pan and instruments and rushed out to hail a cab.

I hustled up to the corner at Lexington Avenue, rudely stepped in front of an elderly woman, and flagged down a yellow cab. It was the morning rush hour, the streets were mobbed, and there was no time for explanations to the woman. Her flair for the well-turned curse followed us for half a block.

"Central Park Zoo," I said, "and could you hurry? I've got to sew up a lion."

The driver nodded, and chalked up his first nut of the day. He looked bored. But he didn't waste any time getting to the zoo.

The park employees were clustered in front of Raunchy's cage, armed with snatch poles. The lion's flanks were splattered with blood, but he seemed active and alert. Many animals differ from humans in their reaction to bleeding.

When I took out the pistol and started loading it, Raunchy froze. It was clear that he was beginning to have second thoughts about our friendship. The tranquilizer dart hit high on the body, but stuck. He circled the cage a few times in half-hearted protest, then growled, curled his lip, and went out.

I cleaned the wound of foreign matter and used heavier thread for the new stitches. There was no internal damage. The closure held and eventually healed.

Lions have very abrasive tongues, and he had simply licked the first set of stitches to shreds overnight. Perhaps it was fortunate that I was leaving for Brazil that weekend. Absence, it is said, makes the heart grow fonder. And the lion, tamer.

For several weeks, I had spent most of my leisure time doing research on the animal life in the Amazonus region. The more I read, the more excited I became about making a trip to the largest unexplored jungle in the world.

Dr. Woods took over the practice with her usual quiet efficiency while I got my act together for the expedition. On Sunday morning, I left from Kennedy Airport, the thirteenth (and final) member of the party.

3

The Gringo and the Anteater

The only way to duplicate the unique taste of Amazon river water would be to drive a herd of camels through your bathtub. Like many North American rivers, it is used as a sewer by all the tribes along its banks. But unlike many North American rivers, it is teeming with all manner of living things.

It was impossible to explain to the natives exactly why we wanted our drinking water boiled. To them that was just another kinky gringo idea. After all, they drank it and seemed immune to the bacteria. But they dutifully boiled it for us, poured it through cheesecloth to remove most of the mud, then used the cheesecloth for other purposes. So if we were anywhere near our base camp in Leticia, Colombia, we packed along a few bottles of soft drinks or beer. A bottle of warm beer in the evening became a symbol of absolute luxury to everyone in the expedition.

With one of the precious bottles in hand, I approached my hammock and tested it carefully before crawling in. We had found that it doesn't take long for things to rot in the rain forest. Rubber disintegrates, leather goods fall apart, metal rusts overnight, and rope shreds in your fingers. Nothing is ever dry, yet you are always thirsty. It would be a lot easier to replace the hammock than the Peruvian beer.

I peeled off my bush jacket, soaked with rain and sweat, and eased in. It was nearing dusk, or what would pass for dusk if one could see through the dense overgrowth. I was looking forward to a brief rest before dinner. Our temporary camp was on one of the million nameless islands that dot the Amazon. Technically we were in Colombia, but I had spent most of the day on the Brazilian side of the river, helping to gather plant specimens.

The expedition was sponsored by the Smithsonian Institute and the University of California as a general ecological survey. Specialists from several related fields had joined it, and I was there because of my interest in the animal life of this virtually unexplored area. But everyone pitched in to help gather data, and everyone worked to survive. We were given some funding and the name of a native guide. Beyond that we were on our own.

It was the dry season. That meant it rained only most of every day. The rest of the year, the rain was endless. We wore standard jungle garb: a thin cotton bushjacket, cotton pants, and shirt. Even our boots were light-weight, as leather or hard-soled hiking boots would have been useless. Ours were made of canvas; the mud fills the pores and partially waterproofs them.

I kept three knives with me: a Swiss penknife that I've had to use for minor surgery more than once, a hunting knife, and a well-balanced throwing knife. I sometimes carry that one at home, too. A vet in Manhattan is not immune to winding up in odd situations.

Relaxing in the hammock, I finished the beer and closed my eyes, feeling nearly human again. The constant rumble of the rain forest, and the chewing and snipping of the insect life that it spawns, began to recede.

A few yards away several of the Berkeley researchers were talking quietly. One of them broke away from the group and approached me. I opened my eyes and tried to smile. "I wasn't really asleep," I said.

She looked upset. "It's too bad about the anteater," she said.

I nodded sleepily. It *is* too bad about the anteater. Even in this natural forest, which covers nearly three million square miles, the anteater faces extinction. But it turned out that she was concerned about a particular anteater, not the species in general.

With tears in her eyes, she explained that some Indians had trapped a giant anteater—a rare animal this far south of Yucatan—and were systematically torturing it to death.

A few commercial tours had stop-offs in Leticia and sometimes ran side trips this far downriver. There was a "nine-to-five" Indian village near our camp, where the natives showed up regularly to sell handicrafts to wealthy tourists. But the village where they actually lived, without the gaudy trappings, was only about a mile away across the river. That's where the trouble was.

If I'd had any inkling of what the next few hours would bring, I'm sure I would have rolled over in the hammock, said "The hell with anteaters!", and gone peacefully to sleep.

The dugout canoe moved sluggishly through the water as we approached the village. Jim and Owe Fullerton, a husband-and-wife research team from our expedition, had volunteered to accompany the guide and myself in an attempt to save the anteater. It was growing darker and we knew we'd have to hurry.

The village was a far cry from the quaint-looking one that the tourists were shown. It was a rough clearing, perhaps fifty yards across, torn from the jungle and dotted with the simplest of wooden shacks.

We pulled up and secured the dugout, expecting no welcome and getting none. Most people who have to make a living the way they do survey strangers with a touch of contempt. Afterhours, anyway.

A dozen men were scattered about near the huts, watching us with guarded interest. Few women were visible. The anteater, looking like something God created after He ran out of ideas for animals, was in a wooden cage in the middle of the clearing.

It was, or had been, a beautiful specimen—deep gray with white-bordered black stripes on each shoulder, nearly six feet long, and weighing fifty-five to sixty pounds. It was obvious that this endangered species was about to have its population reduced by one.

One of his legs looked fractured, his eyes were swollen, and he could barely react to the group of children who were tormenting him. They poked sticks through the bars, punched at him repeatedly with their fists, and when he did not cry out, kicked the cage in anger. He had large, powerful forearms and sharp claws but was beyond the point of fighting back.

Children can be as cruel as adults in any society. Having an animal like this at their mercy seemed to bring out the worst in them. The boys strutted around, shouting and gloating as they attacked, playing at *machismo.*

Three dark-complected natives, dressed in the usual cotton chino pants, blue work shirts, and sandals, stood nearby. They seemed quite unconcerned. The week before, in another village, I'd seen a man split open the stomach of a pregnant lizard for no reason other than to watch it die. Perhaps living in such a harsh and unconquerable environment breeds the desire to strike back at it in some way.

The scene was pitiful. Owe stood there, pale and tight-lipped, and I could see Jim's eyes darting about as he mentally calculated the odds on our survival if trouble arose. I looked at our guide. He shrugged his shoulders, intimating that gringos fare better by minding their own business. He hadn't been exactly thrilled about coming along in the first place.

"Ask them what they're going to do with the animal," I told him.

He approached the three men, hat in hand, and spoke to them carefully and politely in Portugese. The smallest man became quite animated, grinning widely as he talked, and pointing at the cage. The guide nodded and returned.

"They say they're going to sell it to a zoo in the United States and get rich."

You can't get rich on one specimen of giant anteater, even if it's healthy. And this one, if left untreated, would be dead by morning. It sounded like one of those dreams-of-glory schemes, concocted more to break the monotony than anything else.

The children, realizing that several foreigners had joined their audience, doubled their efforts to abuse the crippled beast. It quivered, seeking a protective corner of the cage. One of the children began poking for the eyes with his stick. There's nothing like a little gore to keep an audience amused.

"We ought to do something," said Owe.

"Well, they're sure not looking for advice on animal care," Jim said.

Impulsively, I took a ten dollar bill from my wallet, opened my penknife, and walked over to the cage. The children scattered. Laying the bill on top of the cage, I stuck the knife through it, then said to our guide, "Tell them I just bought the anteater."

I really didn't think there would be a problem. In the economy of the Brazilian jungle, ten dollars is a lot of money. I assumed we would haggle a bit, I'd raise the price to twenty dollars, and everyone would be satisfied.

Unfortunately, I wasn't aware of the fact that the botanist from our party had stumbled across the same scene earlier in the day and had also tried to buy the animal. He'd been informed, quite firmly, that they didn't need any sharpie gringo trying to rip them off, and that the next one who tried it would be fed to the piranhas. Or words to that effect.

The guide translated my rash ultimatum in terms a bit more diplomatic, I'm sure, but the men stiffened. Suddenly the guide was gone, and the three men were strung out in a half-circle around me, their machetes drawn.

I glanced over at the Fullertons. They stood twenty yards from me in the failing light, both their mouths hanging open. The guide was near them, already edging toward the dugout.

It was as though I had stepped into a dream, one of those horrible nightmares full of unimaginable violence that shocks you into wakefulness in the middle of the night. But there was no waking up. I had offended these men, and they sought satisfaction.

Perhaps I could have walked away; apologized, rejoined my friends, and returned to our camp, abandoning the anteater. But I was too stunned to move. No one spoke. Parrots, in flights of dozens, screeched over our heads. Monkeys chattered and scolded, gathering their young before the nocturnal prowlers came out to feed.

Surrounding the dim clearing, the jungle was a solid black backdrop for the senseless little drama. We were in Colombia, with Brazil to our backs, and Peru farther off—not in miles, but in days of travel. How long, I wondered, would it take for news of this transaction in lives to filter upstream to Leticia and on to New York.

The leader's hard brown eyes never left mine. This was his land, his territory, and his village. Even the available weapons were more of his world than mine. Firearms are little more than excess baggage in a rain forest. They rust.

He took a firm step forward, the machete dangling easily in his hand. I could feel the wooden bars of the cage pressing against my back, and the anteater's tail brushing me roughly as it shuffled about.

I unsnapped the sheath that held my hunting knife and pulled it halfway out. The action, I hoped, would make it clear that I was willing to use it. I glanced about. The faces of the children, suddenly silent and engrossed, mirrored the expression of the leader. He leaned forward, just slightly.

I lowered the knife, my hand still on the hilt, and thought, *Okay. He takes one step forward, and we're into it.*

The step came.

How the hell did I get into this?, I wondered, wanting to laugh at the situation, yet knowing at the same time that there was no turning back. The moment for apologies had flashed by. I breathed deeply, trying to relax my body as I drew out the knife.

His mouth opened a fraction as he nodded his head, signalling the others. I tightened my grip on the knife and spread my arms like an old-time gunfighter. I was ready.

He did the last thing I expected. He chuckled. His lips spread wider, and he looked to his friends. They relaxed, returning his grin.

Taking his cue, the children started to laugh. Everyone relaxed, except me.

He sauntered over to the cage and pulled my penknife out of the money. Folding it closed, he handed me the knife and said, "No wonder Americans run the world. Only a gringo would die for an anteater!"

Somewhere in the Amazon rain forest, still alive I'd like to think, is my own personal giant anteater, properly bought and paid for. I may never get back to claim my purchase, but I won't forget how it was made.

The Fullertons helped me fashion a splint for the animal's broken leg, and I treated the superficial wounds and the eyes. The children had drifted back to the cage and watched with mixed reactions.

"What will you do with it?" the leader asked.

"Let it go," I said.

When the guide gave him my answer, the look on his face needed no translation.

After I finished, we moved the animal, grunting and squealing, into our boat and across the river. Untranquilized, he had been difficult to treat, but several of the natives got into the spirit of the thing and helped us hold him down.

A quarter of a mile into the jungle, we located a large hole under a termite-infested tree. There was a stream nearby. He would have plenty to eat and could reach the water easily. An anteater's forearms are larger and more powerful than those of most men, and we felt he would have an even shot at survival. We weren't worried about predators disturbing him. Even jaguars, unless driven by starvation, steer clear of those claws.

We had tied his back legs together so we could drag him through the jungle, but once we wrestled him into the hole, we couldn't get the rope off.

The anteater hunched up, settling in, and wanted no

further part of us. We were all exhausted, drained by a full day in the unrelenting jungle and the confrontation in the village. I wanted to end the affair as quickly as possible, so I climbed down into the hole with the animal. Not a terribly safe thing to do, considering the length and strength of his claws, but it seemed expedient.

Cursing, I pushed the creature around, untying knots as fast as I could, then looked up. Poised above me, set to strike, was a mammoth gray arm. It could have disemboweled me before I could have moved. I closed my eyes and felt the weight of the whole ridiculous day wash over me.

I'd like to think that he held back out of gratitude. But in his eyes, I must have seemed just another hurtful two-legged animal, intent on making his life miserable. He simply chose not to strike, and I scrambled out of the hole, weary and elated. We left him in full darkness and found our way back to camp.

Several days later, we learned that the Ticuna Indian leader had pronounced a ban on hunting anteaters in that area of the jungle. He undoubtedly thought I was a lunatic, and perhaps felt it might bring bad luck to defy my wishes. For whatever reason, his orders would stick. He was greatly respected throughout the territory. He was wanted for murder in Leticia.

4

The Jungle

Some people who live near the subways claim they never hear the rumble of passing trains. The sound becomes so familiar that they are no longer conscious of it. The same mechanism took over as we moved deeper into the jungle. It seemed quiet, but if I stopped to concentrate, I could hear them. The insects.

Billions upon billions of insects chewed and sawed and hacked away at the jungle twenty-four hours a day, yet it was so lush that their labors went virtually unnoticed. Throughout the expedition our entymologist was the busiest man in South America. He identified hundreds of completely new species; for him, every day was like stepping into Creation's experimental laboratory.

One insect that never failed to get a reaction from us

was a gigantic beetle, so heavy that it couldn't fly parallel to the ground. Its backside drooped as it roared down the narrow jungle trails looking like an aerodynamic impossibility. And although it sounded like a truck in high gear, it was in fact a completely harmless creature.

One of the first things I was asked when I returned home (besides "You were in Brazil for a month? Why don't you have a tan?") was if I'd seen any killer bees. They have become a media fad in the past few years, and in the rush to exploit a dramatic situation, the popular press usually leaves recent developments out of the stories. Still, the bees are dangerous and we carefully skirted any areas they had been reported in. In some ways they are like the most savage of dogs—not the watchdog that is trained to attack on command, but the "fear-biter," the dog that strikes for no apparent reason.

Someone had decided to cross the large, vicious African bees with the smaller sucking bees of South America. They hoped to develop a strain of large, nonaggressive, nonstinging bees that would produce more honey. A good idea. And if the experiments had been conducted in Africa, where the vicious bees were already entrenched, it might have worked out well. But they experimented in South America, and—as in the case of the United States boll weevil—some escaped and interbred with the local wild bees.

On a scale of one hundred for hostility and zero for gentleness, the first generation of interbred bees came out close to one hundred. They did indeed produce more honey, but no one in his right mind would try to collect it.

Although there are very few of them in comparison

to the local bees, they breed swiftly and are spreading, moving north at perhaps a hundred miles a year. But their viciousness seems to be diminishing slowly through each generation. They are still nasty and aggressive, but there is hope that these characteristics will be totally absorbed. Maybe nature, in this particular case, will favor the pacifist for a change.

The mosquitoes simply considered the expedition a visit from the Welcome Wagon. We abandoned use of protective netting early in the trip, as it seemed only a minor bottleneck in the cafeteria line of hungry bloodsuckers.

We encountered three different kinds of ants, each, in its own way, a plague. The largest was several inches long and was always seen alone, in pairs, or very small groups. A single bite from one of these giants of the ant world seemed equal to an electrical charge of approximately twenty watts. Several bites would cause more than a casual annoyance. And they were tenacious. I picked one up in a forceps one afternoon, to get a good look at its body structure. It didn't try to escape or shrivel up in defense—it attacked. Swinging, snapping its tail over, biting at me, it was ready to meet the universe nose-to-nose. If all ants displayed this drive for individual survival, we would be engaged in a major war.

Several times we came across swarms of army ants. They are meat eaters that never build nests. Individually, they are quite small, but in colonies of a hundred thousand or more, there is just no way to control them. They flow through the jungle like a river. Near the back of the column, the swarm dwindles down to only a few yards wide, and occasionally we just ran through them, brushing them off our bodies. When it's hot and miserable, and a matter of hiking miles out of your way to get around them, you're willing to take minor chances. Luckily, no one tripped and fell down while crossing.

Once I was getting some close-up photos of insect erosion on a tree trunk, very beautiful and intricate work. And as I moved in closer, about fifty army ants—probably one of their scouting parties—leaped on me and started taking my chest and arms apart. One moment I was peering through the camera, and the next I had been hit with a bucket full of ice water and thumb tacks.

You never travel alone in the jungle, of course. Sam McGinnis, our herpetologist, and Sharon Arce, the field leader of the expedition, wasted no time in helping to rip my shirt to shreds and slap the voracious creatures away. No one made any silly jokes about having ants in one's pants. My skin was dotted with bites for nearly a week.

The rain forest is a tumbling, jumbled world, yet in its depths live probably the most precise creatures on earth. It's a shock to come across a neat path, an inch or so wide, stretching arrow-straight through the undergrowth. This is the work of the leafcutter ants. You can often see hundreds of them, scurrying along their highway, each carrying a twig, a small branch, or a leaf to be used in the construction of their elaborate nests.

I had heard about them. A friend of mine, an anthropologist on a previous expedition, had set up a tent in the jungle. She went off for a few days in the field and when she returned, she found her gear had been stored in exactly the wrong spot. A neat line had been cut through her records and data files. Nothing else had been touched. The edges of the papers fit together perfectly when patched, but the missing inch-wide strip was probably twenty feet underground, adorning the walls of a queen ant's chamber.

Where the leafcutters have had spectacular success, man has failed. The Brazilian government started a mammoth project to build a highway through the rain forest to link the southern and northern provinces. They wanted to move masses of people from impoverished areas to where they could start clearing the jungle for agriculture.

It was started with a big fanfare, but they soon learned that the longer the highway got, the more back-up people they needed. And the longer it took to move supplies, the more food stations were called for. It's a lesson that the invaders of any hostile environment never seem to learn, even though history is crowded with examples.

The human workers, especially those brought in from higher altitudes where the climate is cooler, began to die. Dysentery and malaria took a huge toll as more and more people were moved onto the job. And even as they worked, the road behind them was breaking up because of the climate.

Not everyone in Brazil was in favor of the project, particularly the Indians who lived along the proposed route. Their territory was being taken from them, and they fought back. Or at least the government claimed they did, before strafing their villages from the air. They were killed, intimidated, or driven off. But the jungle wasn't.

If the government had been able to muster the incredible sums of money, resources, and technology to complete the venture, the project might easily have proved to be a disaster for the rest of the world.

Two inches below the topsoil the Amazon basin is sand. You can clear an area and plant crops. But the second year, there is no crop; the nutrients in the soil will have been used up. So many small farms have to keep moving on, clearing other areas, and starting over. On a large scale an irreversible process would be started, and the Amazon jungle—which manufactures nearly a quarter of the world's oxygen—would become a rainless desert.

Initially, the Brazilian food supply (and of course, the population) would increase. But eventually, wherever they planted, there would be desert. It might take a hundred years, but that desert would be self-sustaining and ever-growing, and the devastating results are obvious.

Beyond its contribution to the balance of nature, we got to wondering what the rain forest was worth in dollars and cents. So one day we paced off a rough acre, divided up into four teams, and checked the trees and other flora. When the figures were in, Dennis, our botany expert, estimated that an acre—based on the market value of the trees alone—was worth well over $200,000. The thought of a single project, a single road, leading to the eventual destruction of this vast natural resource was chilling. The Brazilian government has not yet officially given the project up, even though they have been warned that it is nothing more than a highway to oblivion.

We crossed an abandoned stretch of it one afternoon.

The road was broken and overgrown, slowly being reclaimed by the mother jungle. I had the feeling that roads like this must also have been undertaken thousands of years ago to link the fantastic civilizations that flourished and disappeared in South America. And with about the same success.

Although the sounds of the jungle became almost a part of us and went unnoticed much of the time, there was one thing we could never shake off: the feeling of being constantly surrounded by a multitude of life forms. Most of them, such as the jaguar, you never see. Others are glimpsed, momentarily and at a distance, before vanishing into the forest. And some you see too late.

The bushmaster is well named. It is the largest poisonous snake in the Americas, and it looks (and acts) like the rattlesnake's big brother. It varies from six to twelve feet in length, but much as it is feared by the natives, many more deaths occur from the bite of the fer-de-lance.

The fer-de-lance has the nasty little habit of crawling up into the brush and hanging, about face level, over a trail. There are several species of snake that get categorized as the fer-de-lance, some more poisonous than others. But they are all very aggressive, and if they strike from high brush or a low branch, you are apt to get hit in a very dangerous place: near the brain. Usually, the victim is too far into the jungle to reach any kind of medical help in time.

One morning we were moving along a trail and I spotted one lying in front of us. It looked like a small branch, ten or twelve inches long. Just a baby. It didn't strike as I approached and, even though I had a machete in my hand, I picked it up by the tail and tossed it off into the jungle.

Our guide, who had been wary of me ever since the anteater incident, stopped in his tracks. "That snake will grow up and kill someone," he said solemnly and refused to speak to me for the rest of the day.

There are thousands of poisonous snakes in the rain forest and the chances of that particular one ever seeing another human were slim indeed. But talking about statistics was probably irrelevant to someone who had had a member of his family killed by such a snake.

Very little hard information on Amazon wildlife has come out of the jungle. Ecological surveys usually formulate more questions than answers, and we contributed our share. The data we gathered is still being studied at Berkeley; some of it made little sense.

Sam McGinnis was delighted when we discovered a group of caimans—the South American relatives of the alligator and crocodile. They are hard to locate, tending to congregate in small areas along the Amazon tributaries rather than on the big river itself. But we came across a backwater pond that seemed to be a gathering place for them and was perfect for our study.

We camped nearby, on what might be considered high ground, and Sam unpacked his equipment. Under his direction we quietly approached the area and tossed electronic temperature-sensing probes into the pond. Once swallowed, the probes would register blips on an instrument. The caiman eats anything that moves, so there was no problem getting their cooperation.

We concentrated on a dozen animals, recording their body temperatures in the water (which was quite warm), as well as out of the water, in the sun, and in the shade. They were watched carefully. We were trying to determine if they went into the water to raise their temperature, lower it, or just to forage.

At the end of the study, our only conclusion was that some would only go into the water when they were hot, some when they were cold, and others completely at random. They refused to conform to the habits of other amphibians. When we left, still perplexed, I was sure I could detect a few sly snickers in their parting hisses.

No one needed to be told to stay close to camp. You could walk off and get lost fairly easily. At a distance of ten feet, you had difficulty seeing anyone. At fifty feet, you couldn't even hear them. The jungle is just too loud, too dense, and too dark—unless you are on the river, where the sun comes roaring down on you. Our ornithologist, however, went constantly astray.

There is an incredible variety of bird life in Brazil, and he was up and off into the predawn darkness almost every day, alone. Perhaps he had picked up a sort of homing instinct from the birds, for he always managed to find his way back to the campsite.

Early one morning we were loading the canoes and beginning to get worried about him, when he returned with a look of absolute ecstasy on his face. We pushed off and unable to control himself, he began jumping up and down in the canoe.

"Hey, take it easy," someone yelled, "there are piranhas in the river!"

"What do I care? I've got nothing else to live for—I saw *two* king vultures!" He spread his arms to the heavens and looked about ready to take off.

We all became quite close, as any group of people will in unusual and dangerous situations. A friendly rivalry arose between the Berkeley researchers and those of us from the East Coast. We had to take along a fair amount of food with us on long trips into the jungle from Leticia, but we often ran short. Fishing skills became a point of honor.

The California contingent went out with a good deal of bravado, claiming no one on earth could fish like the native Californian. After a full day of luckless casting, they returned with just barely enough food for dinner. Over a meager meal of scrawny and unidentifiable fish, it was suggested that perhaps the California way of fishing might be surpassed.

The gauntlet was down. Charlie Adams and I decided to venture out the next day to represent the Eastern All-Star Anglers. Charlie is a brilliant surgeon who had been on a championship sculling team at college. But the thought of the two of us outfishing our rivals raised a good many eyebrows. Neither of us was much inclined to hunt, either for food or sport.

Our camp at the time was near a Ticuna village, and a troop of children came down to join the bon voyage party. Charlie, the guide, and I manned a fishing dugout and bravely pushed off onto the river. Catcalls from the western contingent and cheers from our eastern fraternity followed us as we moved into the sluggish current and rounded a bend, heading upstream.

I knelt amidship, trying to coordinate my strokes with those of the silent guide in front of me. He exuded the same optimism last seen on the face of the skipper of the Titanic.

Luck is an odd commodity. It can't be weighed, smelled, tasted, touched, and certainly never counted on. Still we insist on its existence. Charlie had spent most of the trip to Brazil plagued by rotten luck, from easily falling off a log to sinking a dugout. I, on the other hand, had escaped every potential disaster. We figured things would have to even out.

As I was trying to decide whether we would strike an iceberg in the lukewarm Amazon or sight a school of smoked salmon, the guide grunted and pointed ahead. Civilization beckoned.

"Land ho!" shouted Charlie, doubling his paddles-trokes and bringing us into a rough collision with a floating log.

A single family of natives had cleared enough jungle away to grow tobacco for trading along the river. We knew that they were friendly, as the women as well as the men and children came over to greet us. They all had the classically beautiful Indian features and welcomed us to their village with a good deal of pride.

The farm was doing quite well, by native standards. But our eyes were riveted elsewhere. Stacked near the river bank, in heaps as high as any of the huts, were mounds and mounds of fresh fish.

"Good God," muttered Charlie, "it's the mother lode!"

A single thought flashed through our minds.

Our guide had a ceremonial chat with the family

patriarch, then told us we had been invited in for a cup of coffee. We agreed eagerly.

The coffee was vile, by any standard whatsoever. We drank it and smiled. Through the guide, we chatted. Their fine weather. Their fine village. And, oh yes, their fine catch of fish. Perhaps they might sell us a few?

The patriarch looked a bit startled, then laughed at our good joke. Why would anyone want to buy something that was so easy to catch? The hardest part of the bargain was convincing them that we were serious, but once convinced, they were more than happy to take advantage of this windfall.

Charlie and I each put in five dollars, and they refused to accept more. One of the family men who spoke a little English offered to deliver two boatloads of fish to the expedition site. We started loading. We'd been out less than an hour and the dugout was brimming with beautiful, shimmering, fresh fish. The native climbed in, preparing to shove off.

"They are going to ask you," I said, "how we managed to catch so many fish. Tell them, 'the New York way,' okay?"

He nodded.

"And tell them, if they need any more, we'll catch another boatload on our way back downstream," added Charlie.

He left, the boat bobbing dangerously low in the water.

We were subjected to a second cup of coffee, graciously offered by the prosperous tobacco farmers.

Charlie was right about the mother lode. When we returned with the final cache, our camp looked like a boomtown in the Old West. But instead of a vein of gold or silver, they had struck fish. Women from the nearby village were carting off huge baskets of them to be seasoned with greens and spices, wrapped in leaves, and roasted. We joined the villagers for dinner that night, had fish again for breakfast, and barbecued fish for dinner the following night.

Charlie and I kept the secret to ourselves, and with rather smug and enigmatic smiles turned aside the avalanche of questions from our awed colleagues. The Berkeley crew took defeat in good grace, but they must have asked us a hundred times, "How do you fish the New York way?"

The expedition—a tiny fleet of dugout canoes—moved along the river well-stocked with smoked fish. We passed a number of nameless villages. They would spring up, flourish, and then be gone within a few years. We saw one, containing perhaps a hundred people, where they had actually set concrete walks into the sand. Such trappings of modern civilization were rare, however.

But because of the traffic along the river, and a free-flowing system of barter, the most unlikely objects sometimes show up in the middle of the jungle.

We were down to drinking boiled river water, laced with halazone tablets, after exhausting a few expensive bottles of beer bought from a government military patrol. The price was high because the sale of military supplies to civilians was an offense punishable by death. But there was a lively market for these supplies, and most patrols were willing to take the risk.

We stopped at a little village to see if they had any sort of canned or bottled beverages to sell. The narrow beach was well trampled, and a few pilings had been driven into the mud just offshore to facilitate tieing up larger craft. It was obviously a popular stop for the river traders.

Immediately after disembarking, we saw the attraction. The natives had gone to a good deal of trouble to build a sturdy-looking shed over what was probably the only pool table within a thousand-mile radius.

There were several cases of beer, canned goods, and other premium products stacked near the shed. We quickly put two and two together. There must be hustlers everywhere in the world, and no matter where you find a pool hall, you are likely to run into someone looking for a fast buck. These villagers lived off the table, hustling fascinated nonplayers out of their bargaining goods.

They never mentioned it. They welcomed us, boiled a ritual cauldron of coffee, and settled in to discuss the unchanging weather. While our guide translated the slow-moving conversation, I got up, wandered around, and ended up near the table. The surface was a faded, blotchy green. It had seen more than one tropical storm, but was anchored in the sandy soil and looked pretty even. The cues were warped and there was no chalk for their shiny ends.

A lone, sharp-eyed native was there, racking up the balls. He had ignored the welcoming ceremonies and seemed intent on positioning the triangle perfectly.

I nodded casually and he returned the nod. I picked up a cue stick and pantomimed a game. He smiled and politely stood back to let me practice and get the feel of his table. He wasn't the head man of the village, but he was obviously in charge of its only industry.

I have a pool table in my New York apartment, but finding time to indulge such a hobby has been difficult over the past few years. I shot poorly. He watched carefully, and I scratched on the fifth ball.

Straightening up, I took out my machete, pointed to it, then to a case of beer, and looked questioning. Language is no barrier in the pool halls of the world. We struck a winner-take-all bargain, and he racked the balls.

People from the expedition and from the village began to drift over to watch. The table was soon ringed by spectators and news of the wager spread. I broke, had a lucky run, and my friends cheered. The prospect of splitting a long-sought case of beer somehow heightened their enthusiasm.

The Indian scratched, and frowned as I took the table again. Attitude at the pool table is as important as the steadiness of the hand. I could just feel that I had the game, but at the same time, I was worried. The delicate balance of a host and guest relationship, as I had learned, can easily turn ugly. The thought of throwing a few points, to make the game closer, crossed my mind.

Lining up the last ball, I looked up at him. His face was a reflection of stoic defeat. I sank the ball, and he motioned toward a case of beer. Before we left, he told me not to feel bad; he would win it back, many times over, from the boatload of tourists that would surely follow in our paths. He drank a bottle with us and wished us well.

We pushed off, heading deeper into the interior. Our idea was not to run the whole 4,000 mile length of the river, but to explore a relatively small section of it in great depth. But before turning back, we entered an area that had rarely been visited by outsiders. Tempered metal was virtually unknown there, but the tribes managed both to hunt and to wage war successfully, fashioning deadly weapons from the lush world around them.

When it is properly processed and administered, curare is a muscle relaxant used in modern medicine. Extracted from plants in a crude, tarlike form, it is a deadly poison. And a dart, dipped into it and fitted into a bamboo blowgun, becomes a lethal weapon in the hands of an expert.

We contacted a tribe rumored to be headhunters, although there was no evidence of such activity when we finally located their village. Other than the scarcity of western-style clothes and machetes, they seemed quite similar to most of the other groups we'd seen. Conversation, however, was impossible. Our guide spoke English, Portugese, and a variety of native dialects, but was baffled by theirs. We used sign language.

Their village, a roughly circular collection of thatched huts, was twenty miles inland from the river. They were polite and reserved and, through gestures, invited us to camp with them. They watched us unpack and were fascinated by our equipment.

I had brought along a battery-powered light, the kind miners wear on their heads. It was supposed to free the hands for night travel in the jungle, but I hadn't found it of much use. I demonstrated it for the chief of the tribe, and he was totally fascinated. I think he felt it was magic. He wanted it.

I am not much of a collector, but when he offered me his spare blowgun and a quiver of curare-tipped arrows, I couldn't refuse. The blowgun was beautiful, intricately carved and stained. I threw in an extra battery and we traded.

My fumbling attempts to operate the three-foot bamboo weapon were met with snickers. They were delighted by my ineptitude. A young man, grinning broadly, took it from me and fitted a dart into the end. The darts were slivers of bamboo, sharpened on one end and widening out to fit snugly into the blowgun. The back end was wrapped in a cottony plant material and sealed the air space.

Casually, he looked around and pointed to a tree that must have been fifty yards from us. I inspected the tree with my binoculars, but could see nothing in it. Laying the blowgun along his outstretched arm he sent a quick but powerful puff of air through it.

A small bird, pierced through the head, fell from the tree. There was no reaction from the tribe. The man had, I gathered, taken an easy shot so as not to lose face in front of foreigners.

We could only spend a day and a half with this tribe of incredible marksmen before heading back for the river. Time was running short; we would soon have to return to Leticia, and on to Bogota for the flight home. I had no way of knowing that I would soon be leaving the expedition to answer an emergency call far downriver.

Four hundred years ago, a Spanish explorer returned to Europe with a pretty wild tale. He claimed that somewhere along Brazil's Maranon river he had encountered a race of fair-skinned, blonde, women warriors. Harking back to an old Greek legend, he called them Amazons. He must have been a convincing storyteller, as the Maranon was renamed Amazon, and the tale of the warrior women persists.

I met one. Or at least someone who could pass for one. Diana Majors was fair skinned and blonde, and she was indeed a warrior. She was fighting against the eventual, perhaps inevitable, extinction of a species endangered by man: the manatee, a gentle and intelligent aquatic mammal.

Diana, supported by a small grant from the Canadian government, lived on a houseboat on the river. Whenever she heard reports of manatee sightings, she traveled hundreds of miles to check them out. Even though the manatee is protected by law, few human scavengers would turn down fifteen hundred pounds of edible meat, usable oil, and hides.

She became quite well known along the Amazon, and her persistence finally paid off. She found a manatee. Two of them, in fact. And shortly thereafter, a message reached our camp: Is there a veterinarian in the group?

A female manatee had been harpooned and had already died. The baby, though wounded, was still living. I left the expedition and hurried down to offer what aid I could.

She welcomed me to the village, far from her houseboat base, where the baby manatee was being kept in a water pen. She was quite gracious and was relieved to see me, even though I admitted I'd never treated a manatee before.

The baby, only a week old, was about one meter long and weighed twenty-five pounds. It looked like a rather large loaf of French bread before it's baked. It had a fan-shaped flipper at one end, two smaller flippers and a bristly snout at the other, and large, liquid eyes. The wound was ghastly looking. It had also been harpooned, but no vital organs had been injured. After treating the superficial damage, I stayed on several days for observation. It was remarkably gentle and friendly.

The manatee is a harmless creature, actually one of man's few allies in the animal kingdom. They feed on vegetation that would ordinarily block waterways. In Florida, they've been stocked in some canals that have become overgrown due to the dumping of phosphates and detergents, a process which deoxygenates the water, causing everything to die except the weeds. The manatees do a good job of clearing the canals, but they are very slow moving and motorboats chop their backs to pieces.

Even in aquariums most of the manatees have five or six scars on their backs if they've lived in the wilds for any length of time. The sad thing is, the manatee is an intelligent animal. Once hit by a motorboat's propellers, it understands what has happened, and the second time it realizes what will happen, but just can't move fast enough to get out of the way.

After I returned to the United States, I got a letter from Diana. The manatee had improved, and she wanted to float it down a long stretch of the Amazon to her houseboat for study. But she would need several air mattresses to do it and they were unobtainable down there.

An unflappable Sears and Roebuck saleslady took my order and asked where I'd like the air mattresses shipped.

"To Miss Diana Majors," I said.

"Address?"

"Somewhere along the Amazon river, in Brazil," I said.

She calmly wrote it down and completed the paperwork. I suppose that, over the years, Sears has handled a goodly number of rather unique orders.

Just as I got home, the phone rang. It was the Sears office manager. Unfortunately, he explained, Sears would be unable to deliver a package to some vague spot along a river that is four thousand miles long. Could I be a little more specific? Well, no. Well then, he was worried. Well, so was I. The manatee was stranded up the river without a mattress.

It seemed worth a try, so I bought the mattresses in a department store, wrapped them up, and mailed them. Miraculously, they arrived. The Brazilian postal department must be a hardy lot.

We corresponded for awhile, and Diana kept me up to date on the manatee's progress. From time to time she asked for medical advice. It took a good deal of research to come up with suggestions, but the last I heard the animal was thriving and never strayed far from wherever she happened to be. A real houseboat pet.

Taking a shower in the jungle is simple. You find a clearing, strip, suds yourself with soap, and wait for it to rain. That usually doesn't take very long.

I caught up with the expedition two days travel from

Leticia. A large body of data had been gathered, and while we were anxious to begin evaluation, the daily triumph over the challenge of survival had become invigorating in a way that few city dwellers ever experience.

There had been a run of freaky weather in the area. For several days it rained only at night, or very early in the morning, or when the expedition was on the move, and no one had a chance to get decently washed. One minute's perspiration was flooded away by the next, and it got to the point where peeling off your soaking clothes became a task.

I decided I couldn't stand it any longer. When the smell of your own sweat keeps you from sleeping, you do something about it. I saw some Indians, fishing by their little dugout across the river, and thought it would be refreshing to swim over to them and back. I stripped, sudsed myself up, and dived into the lukewarm Amazon.

As I swam toward them, I kept feeling things banging into me; debris, I assumed, floating downstream. But I continued, pausing only to return the waves of the Indians, who had stopped fishing to watch.

I pulled myself up into their canoe and shook like a wet dog, enjoying the feeling of being—at least temporarily—clean. The Indians stared at me for a moment, then went back to hauling in fish. They handled the fish carefully. The fish were piranhas.

In Brazil, it is considered impolite to pass out in your neighbor's canoe. I came close. Piranhas eat anything that moves, and these were big piranhas, most of them over a foot long. I didn't know they got that big. I didn't know their teeth got that big, either. They are attracted to the scent of blood. If I'd had a scratch or cut of any kind on my body, or if they had felt a little more antagonistic, I wouldn't have made the first ten strokes.

The Indians agreed to ferry me back to the other shore. I had somehow lost my desire for an afternoon swim. It was the sort of thing everyone laughed about afterwards, but no one in the expedition, I noticed, went near the water until we reached Leticia.

Reluctantly, we worked upriver to Leticia, and then on to Bogota. Creature comforts like air conditioning and drinkable water were welcome, of course, but behind us were a million unanswered questions about the nature of life in the jungle. We felt like the fabled blind men, each touching a different part of an elephant, then trying to describe it. But describing a hypothetical elephant and dealing with a real one that had gone berserk were, I was soon to learn, two different things.

5
Eight Tons
of Trouble

Julia had a fan club. Nice people showed up at the Central Park Zoo nearly every day for years, just to feed her peanuts and admire eight tons of gentle elephant. Many of them had no pets of their own and just sort of emotionally adopted her. Such a concern for animals may be only natural in man and emphasizes the real need for city zoos. It can also lead to tragedy.

I had hoped to take a few days off after the Amazon expedition to rest, unpack, see a few friends, and reacquaint myself with life on a different—if no less hectic —level. Bags in hand, I checked in with the office. Dr. Woods, Bill, and Caroline, under the careful scrutiny of our menagerie, had things running quite smoothly. I went upstairs to my apartment. Barnaby, who had spent most of the past month being shamelessly spoiled by the office staff, hit me like a ton of sheep dog. And the phone was ringing.

It was the Central Park Zoo. John Fitzgerald, a zoo-keeper, had been attacked by one of the animals and was in the hospital with a badly damaged lung.

"What happened?"

"Julia nearly killed him."

There was a grim irony to the situation. Julia owed her life to John Fitzgerald, the tall, gentle man who had been her friend for years. Zoo animals often develop a close relationship with one particular keeper, and John seemed to be Julia's favorite. John treated her with understanding and patience, and she responded in kind. An African elephant with beautiful, unmarred tusks, she grew to maturity in Central Park and had a loyal following.

Then one day, several years ago, she suddenly grabbed an elephant pole out of another keeper's hands, smashed it into little pieces, and threw it at him. An elephant pole is a long sturdy stick with a blunted hook on its end. It looks wicked, but to an animal stronger than ten automobiles, it's like a straw. It would be impossible to scratch an elephant hard enough to draw blood with one.

The keeper jumped out of the way and stood, shocked, staring up into one of her mild eyes. There was no hint of anger there. She went back to the domesticated, slow-moving habits of a zoo-raised pachyderm.

A week later, John began to feel a growing nervousness in the beast. There was no change in her behavior patterns, but a lifetime of working with animals had honed his sensitivity to their moods. Her gradually shifting attitude surfaced slowly. Within the month, she threw her first temper tantrum and attacked the other elephant in the enclosure with no provocation.

For the safety of the patrons as well as the park employees, she was isolated. The fits of temper became more frequent, almost as if she was reverting to a wild state. Reports circulated in the Parks Department, conferences were held, and somewhere up the chain of authority, it was decided that she would have to be euthanized.

John disagreed. He felt that, with careful handling, she could be quieted down and brought back into line. But the proclamation stood, and it looked like his friend of many years was doomed. So he went to the public.

He wrote and circulated a petition, which was signed by many hundreds of people, demanding that Julia's life be spared. Public interest was aroused and a stay of execution was issued. Julia rewarded him by attempting to kill him.

Most of our attitudes toward elephants stem from the tales written by Rudyard Kipling or the movies of Alexander Korda. They are thought of as large, gray creatures, standing throughout history at man's side, ever ready to help him with his conquest of the world around him. But because of this gentle-good-and-wise image, we tend to forget that an elephant must be treated firmly. You can't roll up a newspaper, swat it, say "Naughty elephant!", and expect it to react like a house pet. And once an elephant gets the notion that its keeper or trainer might not represent absolute authority, rebellion is sometimes the result.

Julia was probably handled too gently. It may sound ridiculous, but a keeper has to push an elephant around roughly. Viewed from the other side of the fence, it might look like animal abuse. Observing this, well-meaning citizens sometimes call the newspapers or the Humane Society and complain. A furor arises, and the Parks Commission reacts like the next domino in line. An order is issued: Quit picking on the elephants.

Julia went rogue.

An angry elephant's manner of dealing with humans is simple and direct. It usually knocks a man down, kneels beside him, then crushes him to death with its forehead. You can't argue with that kind of efficiency.

John was working in the enclosure, and Julia seemed quite normal. Then, as he turned his back on her, she swung her massive trunk and brought it crashing down on his head. He fell heavily, but did not lose consciousness. As he rolled over on his back, he saw Julia ponderously sink to her knees, carefully place her forehead on his rib cage, and begin to apply pressure. It had only taken a few seconds, but by the time Julia had settled beside him, zoo visitors were screaming.

Attendants came rushing from every direction, and the first few to arrive dashed into the enclosure. They attacked the elephant, flailing away with anything at hand, punching her with their fists, shouting, trying to divert her attention from John.

John Fitzgerald is a large and well-muscled man in excellent physical shape. That fact, plus the speed of his fellow keepers, saved his life. Julia rose and turned on her attackers. Another keeper dodged around her and dragged John to safety. Amid the confusion, someone ran to the zoo office and called for an ambulance.

On ninety-nine out of every hundred summer days, a stroll through Central Park Zoo is a pleasant experience. John was felled, before a horrified audience, on the hundredth day. I got home on the hundred-and-first.

I hoped that there might be some physical ailment causing Julia's personality change. She could no longer be considered merely cantankerous, and the thought of what might happen if a parent lifted a child over the bars to feed the elephant called for immediate action.

Outwardly, she appeared normal, meandering casually around the enclosure and, because of her great size, seemingly stoic. But there was something in her eyes. She was more observant of every move made in the vicinity. If anyone approached, her trunk would raise—sometimes only slightly, but always prepared to strike.

She glared as I swung over the bar that separated her cage from the reach of the public. I kept moving, the loaded tranquilizer pistol in hand, jockeying for a clean shot. Her ears spread instinctively to help pinpoint my exact whereabouts. Scuttling to the side, I put a shot of anesthetic into her exposed shoulder. Once she collapsed, I took blood samples for analysis and ran a complete physical study. Julia, we learned, was healthy.

During the following week, she continued the threatening gestures toward humans and bullied the other elephant mercilessly. The keepers were, understandably, fearful of entering the cage. Her food was dumped through the back of the elephant house and an attendant was posted outside the open-air enclosure to warn the public. It was clear that she would have to be destroyed.

The news media quickly got into the act. There was a televised meeting with the Parks Commissioner, and the future of this dangerous animal became a much debated issue.

In many cities of the world, such an incident would go unnoticed. The public would show up one morning, and there would just be one less elephant. But in New York, we had to buck public opinion from the moment euthanasia was decided upon clear through the bizarre post-mortem. The commissioner was condemned as being heartless, and several organized groups demanded that Julia be given to an animal sanctuary. The fact that she was much too wild, and would endanger any animals around her, seemed to make no difference.

Despite a tide of indignant protests, a team was assembled to handle the job. Bunnie Brook of the Sanctuary for Animals, Dr. Strebel representing the New York Medical Center, and two vets: Dr. Umphenhour and myself. Our first problem was simply location. Could Julia be moved to a less visible place before being euthanized? We met, discussed it, and decided probably not. We would have to work in the elephant house. That brought up another problem: what do you do with a dead elephant? You can't leave a carcass that size just lying around. We began to feel like assassins.

I suggested that we find a likely glen right there in Central Park, erect a small statue over the grave, and call it "The Elephant's Graveyard." An educational display could be worked out, admission charged, and the money used to help cover costs of running the zoo. The proposal was voted down. We contacted the Department of Sanitation and explained the situation. The assignment was a bit out of the ordinary, but they showed up on the appointed day with a crew of men, a large open-topped truck, a giant crane, and half a dozen power saws.

Julia was more nervous than usual, picking up our tension, perhaps, from the air. She moved just as I shot, and the hypodermic dart barely seemed to pierce the thick, leathery skin on her haunch. Several minutes passed before she began to weave.

We stood, watching silently. She broke into a lumbering trot around the enclosure, then sank to her knees for the last time and rolled over on her side.

We entered the cage, hooked up an intravenous tube, and started pumping a massive volume of barbiturate into her. It takes quite a large dose to euthanize an elephant. One cubic centimeter would be enough for a ten-pound dog. Julia weighed eight tons. Nearly an hour passed before we were sure she was dead.

The post-mortem took hours. We had to dress in boots, slickers, and rain hats borrowed from the Fire Department. We were soon drenched in blood. The image of Jonah and the whale kept recurring to me as I stood inside the animal, looking up under the ribs, trying to locate the kidneys. It was a chance to study elephant anatomy that few of us would ever have again, and the excitement of learning kept us going far beyond the point of exhaustion.

The stench became overpowering and Bunnie went to open the door. As it swung open, a hundred flashbulbs exploded. Central Park was swarming with amateur photographers, come to capture the elephant autopsy. They were perched in trees or atop nearby buildings, anywhere that might afford a better view. The police chased them away. They returned in droves. When the distraction got to be too much, we had to close the doors.

Well after midnight, the Department of Sanitation team moved in and sectioned the carcass with their power saws. The crane rolled into place, and lifted huge pieces over the fence and into the truck.

Julia was buried in a Brooklyn landfill, without ceremony or notice in the papers. Imagine the questions this will pose for future archaeologists as they sift through a strata of twentieth century condominium rubble.

A more detailed analysis of Julia's body only strengthened the earlier diagnosis. Her problems had been psychological rather than physical. That should have ended the incident, unhappy as it was; but there were unforseeable repercussions.

There is a pecking order, even among the largest of mammals. Once Julia was gone, the elephant that she had attacked and dominated so completely began to feel his oats. He has since injured several keepers.

As soon as his antisocial reactions started to surface, I tried to have him moved. If he could be taken to a place where circuses winter their elephants, he would be in the hands of specialists. The company of tamer elephants, I thought, might bring him around. But the city government, quite understandably in view of the furor Julia caused, is reluctant to get rid of two elephants within a year.

Trouble with elephants is not rare. Even though they have been studied in captivity and in the wild, there is no great body of information available regarding their medical treatment.

A few years ago, one of the other zoo elephants was showing all the symptoms of having worms. I called around to various vets for advice. No one seemed quite sure about what to do, but along the way I picked up a collection of elephantine oddities and superstitions. A vet from one of the major zoos in America suggested that I grind up a giant wad of chewing tobacco and feed it to the creature. It would, he assured me, kill the parasites. I'm sure it would. Nicotine is a poisonous drug, and if you feed any animal enough of it, even hardy parasites like worms would die. The F.D.A., however, takes a dim view of nicotine as a cure for anything.

This and other wait-until-there's-a-full-moon type of advice was no help. Left to my own devices, I reasoned that an elephant is just, basically, a horse with a long nose. I medicated him accordingly, and the worms disappeared.

The exchange of information, particularly among zoo vets, is a free-flowing and many-sided conversation. The medical problems at one zoo today can easily crop up at another zoo tomorrow, and everyone in the field seems as eager to learn as to teach. The person I usually rely on when I'm stuck is Emil Dolensek of the Bronx Zoo. He has been at it a good many years and is practically a walking encyclopaedia of rare animal ailments.

San Diego has one of the great zoos of the world, and the staff there is top notch. They have always been understanding of my situation—trying to service three zoos on a part-time basis—and have always been helpful. Except for the time I encountered my first (and only) case of elephant pox.

The Sanctuary for Animals in Colts Neck, New Jersey, is a haven for hundreds of unfortunate creatures. From stunted lions to crippled horses to that rarest of animals, a *good-natured* camel, named George. It is run by Len and Bunnie Brook, two people I am very proud to know, and often work with. To finance the Sanctuary, they formed the Dawn Animal Agency. Many of the animals appearing in Broadway shows are owned or handled by them, including those with the New York City Opera.

They called one day and announced that they had just obtained a young elephant. It was scheduled to appear shortly in an animal show and exhibit in Madison Square Garden, but had suddenly taken ill. I drove out to Colts Neck to examine it.

The elephant was a baby, standing shoulder-high, and weighing less than a thousand pounds. Bunnie had been feeding it by hand from a gallon bottle fitted with a gigantic rubber nipple. Naturally, it assumed that she was the mother. It followed her everywhere and was settling rapidly into the routine of a farm that substituted penguins for chickens and cheetahs for house cats. Then it started disgorging, became weak and rheumy looking, and quit eating.

I diagnosed some sort of food poisoning—salmonella, perhaps—and treated it with antibiotics. It started eating immediately but within a week developed skin lesions similar to smallpox. Several of the sanctuary workers who had handled the elephant came down with strange sores on their hands. I began to wonder if this could be a variation of smallpox, such as cows used to have and which rendered milkmaids immune when the plague swept through Europe. There is very little vaccine around. It's just not required anywhere in the world today, except perhaps in Ethiopia.

I got on the phone and called every vet I knew who had treated baby elephants. There aren't many of them. The vet at the Portland Zoo had heard of rare cases of elephant pox before, but the people in San Diego were baffled. Most of the vets asked to be kept informed of the developments. I wasn't able to supply further information.

The condition simply cleared up, in both the workers and the elephant, for what reason we'll probably never know. That's the trouble with exotic animal diseases; even if you come up with a treatment that seems to work, there's always the possibility that the animal would have gotten well anyway.

The show opened at the Garden with a healthy young elephant. Healthy, young, and strong. They didn't want to put chains on the legs of a baby, so the awkward little creature was kept inside a fence. Several people were stationed around the fence, and every time it looked like the elephant was going to lean on it, they moved it. He was very friendly and gravitated naturally toward people. But no one wanted him to get the idea that he could wander freely around Madison Square Garden, sampling popcorn and creating stampedes.

Young animals need exercise, and the Brook's elephant got more than his share each night, after the show closed. Bunnie took to jogging through the darkened halls with the obedient baby thundering at her heels.

Quite recently, I got into the elephant business myself. Dr. Woods had left the practice and moved to New England to get married. My new associate, Dr. Stan Gorlitsky, hadn't started yet, and I was handling the office alone.

Things were backing up. I had regular clients to see, several surgeries to perform, a trip to the Flushing Zoo to make, and I was still flirting with the idea of getting in a little afternoon tennis. But somehow, I had the feeling that my doubles partners were going to be sore at me once more. They had even started arranging for five people to play in our foursome and had assured the other person he would get to play nine times out of ten.

The first couple of times I was either late or couldn't show up at all, they were amused with my excuses. A date with an ailing gorilla. A pregnant zebra developing sudden complications. But it's amazing how even the most bizarre excuses get to be old hat. It had reached the point where, whenever I called, they would say, "You'd better be in the hospital, or don't even bother to tell us why you're missing the game!"

I was between operations when Bunnie Brook called. She's a busy lady and never calls just to say hello. I knew that either there was a political development on the Endangered Species Bill, or she had an emergency at the sanctuary. Only one thing was for sure: no matter what she called for, the solution would not be speedy or simple.

I took the phone, mentally rifling through my Tennis Cop-Out File.

Bunnie got right to the point. It seems there was this cute little baby elephant, and—

"It's sick again?" I asked.

"This is a different one," she said and continued. It was owned by a circus that didn't have the world's greatest facilities for large animals. Quarters were cramped, and the baby was doomed to spend most of its life in unpleasant surroundings. But the owners of the circus had agreed to sell it.

Bunnie had managed to raise about half the money needed to buy it. "Have you ever thought," she said, "about how neat it would be to own an elephant?"

I hadn't.

"Look at it this way. How many people on your block have one?"

I looked at it that way. There were, I had to admit, very few elephants in the Murray Hill section of Manhattan. And I could probably fit a smallish one through the front door and out into the back yard. But if I kept it there for only two or three months, the only way it could get out would be to walk through the house and out the front wall.

"Of course I want an elephant," I said. "Everyone wants an elephant."

"Fine. I'll tell the guy we're buying it together. Half-owners, okay? One of my daughters will be in to pick up your check tomorrow."

"Maybe we should keep it at your place," I suggested.

"Good idea. After we bring it in to the office for a checkup."

"Will it fit?"

"It's small," she said. "And, by the way, leave the check blank. I'm not sure how much it's going to be."

"Naturally."

She hung up.

We bought the elephant, and the Brooks brought it in. We had two cats, a parrot, three dogs, two lizards, a bobcat, and all their owners in the office. When I stuck my head out into the waiting room and yelled, "Bring in the elephant!", our regular clients moved quietly and politely aside.

Elephants have not always spelled trouble for me. One of them even saved me the cost of a speeding ticket.

A small circus was encamped out on Long Island, and we got an emergency call from them on a Friday night. I grabbed a bag and started out.

Weekend travel on the Long Island Expressway is usually murder. It is snowswept during the winter and jammed to a crawl in the summer. The circus owner had a sick elephant on his hands, and I was anxious to get to the scene. But traffic bottlenecked. Everyone in the western hemisphere seemed to be headed for Montauk Point.

I moved three miles in the first thirty minutes. So I pulled off to the shoulder, geared up, and added another lane to the Expressway. As I rounded a corner, I saw a multitude of flashing lights from a parked Highway Patrol car. A grim-lipped patrolman motioned me over, and I pulled up beside him.

"Got a license?"

I looked him right in the sunglasses and said, "Would you believe I'm visiting a sick elephant?"

He paused. His expression didn't change, but he paused. "Get in line," he said. There was a line of cars that had tried the same thing I had. Another officer was methodically writing out tickets for them. I got in line.

Several minutes passed before the patrolman I had spoken to returned. He sighed and rested his arm on my rolled-down window. I suppose he had heard every imaginable excuse from lawbreakers.

"Sick elephant, right?"

I nodded.

"On the off chance . . . that you . . . just might . . . be telling the truth . . . I'm gonna let you go."

"Thank you," I said.

"And if I don't see anything about a sick elephant in the newspaper," he added, "you'd better keep your ass off the Long Island Expressway."

6
George Camel

The Moscow Circus opened at Madison Square Garden late in 1975. The rotunda on Eighth Avenue was filled with thousands of people for every performance. At that time, in that place, George Camel began masturbating.

Prior to that time he had been considered a rarity among camels: he had a pleasant disposition. Bunnie Brook had raised him from a baby on her New Jersey farm, and he just never learned the nasty little tricks that other camels employ to communicate their displeasure. Even a well-trained camel will occasionally kick, bite, or vomit at people. But not George.

The promoter at Madison Square Garden was familiar with the humanitarian work of the Brook Sanctuary for Animals, and offered Len and Bunnie a space in the rotunda. People who come to the circus, he reasoned, are interested in animals and might want to contribute to this worthy cause. The Brooks, naturally, jumped at the chance.

They contacted me several weeks before the show opened and asked if I'd like to help out. A veterinarian experienced in treating large animals had already donated his time, but they needed someone to handle basic problems with the smaller ones. I agreed.

I was not a zoo vet at the time and had never treated, in any official capacity, large exotic animals. My practice consisted of house pets, with an occasional ocelot or raccoon thrown in. Knowing how and when to anesthetize larger animals is practically a different field, and many vets won't get involved with it at all. To a metropolitan-based vet like myself even the treatment of horses and cows was in the exotic category.

Every performance by the Moscow Circus was packed from Thanksgiving through Christmas. The Brooks had brought in a good many of their nice, friendly animals, and had set up booths, exhibits, and a camel ride. George was an instant hit, and there was always a long line of people waiting to climb between his shaggy humps and trot around the Garden, waving to their friends. He was nearly full grown, about seven feet tall from hoof to hump, and beautifully behaved.

Things went smoothly and the animals seemed to thrive on the attention paid them by visitors. The other vet and I made visits to the rotunda almost every day to check on the animals, but when Christmas week rolled around, he left town for the holidays. Almost immediately, George started acting up.

He became cantankerous, and a cantankerous camel is one of the most unpleasant creatures on earth. Besides kicking and biting, he can also regurgitate fermenting food from his stomach with great accuracy, within a range of about ten feet. The stench is unbelievable.

George was much too cultured to resort to such ends. One day he was nervous, the next he began breaking through his pen, and the third he assaulted a female elephant. That can be quite fatal, for a camel. He started masturbating, lowering his penis and smashing at it with his hoof over and over again. The Brooks, of course, had closed the camel ride. The other vet was out of town, so they called me for aid.

"It's Mrs. Brook," said Caroline, handing me the phone.

"Hi, Bunnie."

"Mike, you've got to do something about George Camel," she said, "you've seen how he's getting."

"I'm just not qualified. I've never handled a camel. The only thing I know about camels is that Lawrence of Arabia used to ride around on one."

She paused, then said, "Well, I don't know what to do. Maybe it's the mating season—don't they get irritable when they're in rut?"

I tried to recall what I knew of the genus *Camelus.* It was sketchy, at best. "I think so. But his change seems pretty drastic. I'll call around and see what I can find out. Maybe we can get someone to come in."

"Please, Mike," she said, "you know how we feel about George."

I knew. He had been their particular pet for several years and roamed the sanctuary at will with his friends, a small herd of horses. More than one car has veered sharply off the road when it passed the farm, as the driver spotted a herd of peacefully grazing horses—with two humps and a majestic head jutting up from its midst.

I don't have a private office or consultation room. We're much too busy to bother with such formalities. I dragged a chair up beside Caroline's desk and started working my way through our card file of names and phone numbers.

Zoo vets seemed to be the logical place to start. All of them had camels. None of them had ever heard of a masturbating camel, and few had ever even anesthetized one. The large-animal vets in private practice all backed off after I'd described the symptoms. Finally I began calling veterinary colleges, feeling that there must be someone who—out of sheer curiosity if nothing else— would want to get involved with the case.

A professor at a large eastern university agreed to try diagnosis and treatment if we would bring the camel to the campus. That, I said, could be arranged. I hung up, relieved. For two hours, I had been backing toward a decision that I didn't want to make.

I was about to call Bunnie with the good news, when the phone rang. It was the professor. He had had second thoughts. It was too risky. Sorry.

I canceled the rest of the morning appointments, grabbed a coat, and walked out the front door. It was snowing. The wind whipped up Lexington Avenue as I turned the corner and headed toward Thirty-fourth Street. It was a long walk to Madison Square Garden, but I thought that trudging about in the dead of winter might help clear my head. Christmas was over, New York City was threatening to close up shop because of the latest fiscal crisis, the weather was rotten, and the people I passed on the streets seemed altogether too cheerful.

The walk cooled me off, to be sure, but otherwise only delayed my facing the situation. The main rotunda was darkened when I entered. The Moscow Circus had the night off, but there was a rock concert scheduled in the smaller Felt Forum.

Two of the Brooks' handlers were sweeping up near the exhibits as I passed. We exchanged nods and I went over to sit down beside George's pen.

The other animals were quiet, and even George seemed relatively at peace. The face of a camel—except to those who work with them constantly—is expressionless. There was no way I could judge his mood, although I assumed he was in some pain. He had kicked at his penis until it was raw and looked infected.

I sat for several hours, weighing my responsibility as a veterinarian against my inadequacy to diagnose the problem and treat the animal successfully. I felt very small, sitting there in that massive, darkened building, with my head in my hands.

This camel had been raised by very dear friends of mine, and I knew that attempting the wrong treatment could be worse than no treatment at all. But I had been on the scene from the beginning, and if I refused to at least try to help, no matter how inexperienced I was, I would be violating both friendship and a commitment to life.

There was no alternative. I had to try.

I was back at the office in time for the afternoon patients. Between shots and surgeries, I called the Brooks, told them about my luckless inquiries, and that I was willing to try to anesthetize him that evening and treat his superficial wounds. We arranged to meet at the Garden at ten o'clock. I had several hours of research ahead of me and also needed some time to locate an anesthetic. M-99, from what I had heard, would be perfect. But it is a carefully controlled drug, and you have to be a zoo vet to obtain it. I called the Bronx Zoo. Dr. Dolensek was out of town, and no one else was authorized to release any of it. They were sympathetic and understanding but explained that the drug was in short supply everywhere. Even if they cut through the red tape, it might take as long as three weeks to get any from the manufacturer.

I estimated the camel's weight, and prepared an injection of a more familiar anesthetic. From my hasty research on camel physiology and behavior, I learned that 1) he was not in rut, and 2) camels do not masturbate.

Bunnie and the handlers were there when I arrived and Len was on his way in from New Jersey. We decided to go ahead and entered the pen. Bunnie began talking to the camel in a quiet, friendly tone. He was skittish. One of the handlers got hold of his harness. I gritted my teeth and hit a vein with the anesthetic. We watched him carefully. No reaction. Thirty seconds ticked by. Then suddenly he was down, in a tangle of awkward-looking legs.

I jammed a stethoscope against his ribs, held my breath, and listened. Not a murmur. I looked up at Bunnie. "He's dead," I said.

Bunnie is the kind of woman who can handle almost any kind of emergency, but the loss of George Camel was too great a shock. She fainted.

Meanwhile, the rock concert had just ended at the Felt Forum and hundreds of young people came pouring out. The police tried to keep them moving, but many stopped at the sanctuary exhibit. The air was reeking with the smell of marijuana. People started yelling and pointing to the fallen figures, and there I stood: my first camel, dead, and one of my closest friends, unconscious.

Leonard Brook came elbowing through the crowd and immediately wanted to know why his wife and his camel were on the ground.

Before I could open my mouth, one of the handlers yelled, "Mike! George's eye twitched!"

I grabbed a bottle of smelling salts from my bag, handed it to Len, nodded toward his wife, then leaped on the camel.

The kind of cardiac massage I had used on smaller animals would be no more than a tickle to a creature the size of George. I had to sit on his chest with my feet touching the floor, then jump up in the air and let the full force of my buttocks come down on his rib cage. Repeatedly.

He gasped. His eye twitched again. There was scattered applause from the ever growing crowd of teenagers. Len brought Bunnie out of her faint and told her that I was working on George, that there was a chance he might be saved.

I began to sweat, not knowing whether I had injected an incompatible drug or had simply overdosed him. I kept jumping rhythmically until I was almost exhausted, then Len took over. Three minutes was about the limit for that sort of activity, so we organized shifts. The handlers took turns while we rested, and several onlookers volunteered. After two or three turns apiece, we were glad to accept help. The only rule was, you had to be over a hundred and fifty pounds to apply. You needed weight to be of any effect at all.

When his breathing steadied and his heart rate returned to near normal, I cleaned, treated, and sutured his infected member. The crowd had thinned considerably. It was nearly four o'clock in the morning. We were all dead tired and would carry bruises on our rumps for a week, but George was alive.

He was returned to the farm and recuperated. I fashioned a cup to protect his genital area, but his difficult temperament was unchanged. Further treatment was indicated—but treatment for what?

Mohammed was an old friend of mine, a vet who had graduated from the University of Cairo. He was in town shortly after New Year and dropped by the office to renew our acquaintance. Here, I thought, was a windfall. Who better to diagnose a camel than an Egyptian veterinarian? We went to lunch, then back at the office I described George's symptoms.

"We don't use camels," he said, "we use jeeps. Camels are for tourists. Around Cairo anyway."

"But there are some around?"

"Sure, there's some around. For cigarette commercials and trips to the pyramids."

"Well, what do you do when one starts acting like George?" I said, "I can't find any information on it, and he just keeps getting worse."

"Simple," said Mohammed. "Shoot him."

I attended a veterinary conference in mid-January and, by sheer luck, ran into Dr. Evans, a very brilliant specialist in the field of weird and exotic animal anatomy. We got to talking and, of course, I brought up George. He was as baffled as I, but remembered that in his library he had two books that might shed some light on the mystery ailment. One was on camels in general, written in 1931, and the other concerned unusual glandular activity in large mammals. Not exactly the kind of books a vet keeps around for ready reference. He offered to research the case, and I described George's symptoms in detail.

Two days after the conference ended, Dr. Evans called me in New York. He had discovered that northern antelopes and some types of deer had been known, on occasion, to develop a rare gland located behind the ears. It had only been documented a few times. The gland secreted a black, oily fluid that caused supersexual activity in the animal. Little else was known about it and, besides the obscure references that Dr. Evans found, no further inquiry has been made into the nature of this odd gland.

The symptoms seemed to match. Dr. Dolensek was back in town, and I was able to get enough of the proper anesthetic to attempt an operation. The questionable gland was there, and I removed it.

George Camel regained both his health and his gentle disposition, and I was suddenly an expert on the treatment of large and exotic animals. The New York City Parks Department became interested in me as a candidate for the position of zoo veterinarian. I went to work hard to qualify for the job.

7
The Bad News Bears in Brooklyn

In the Spring of 1977, plumbing problems cropped up at the Central Park Zoo. The pool in one of the bear enclosures was clogged and, if left to stagnate, could be a health hazard for the three elderly bears that lived there.

Making house calls is the plumber's stock in trade. But making a den call is something else again. The bears would have to be relocated before the pools could be drained and the maintenance work done.

At just that time the Prospect Park Zoo in Brooklyn happened to have very nice, and very empty, facilities for bears. What could be more logical than bundling up the bears and moving them out there? But the Prospect Zoo was twenty miles from Central Park. They would have to be trucked past millions of people and thousands of cars, and they were not the lovable honey-hunters so often seen in the movies. They were grizzlies.

The grizzly is a subspecies of that giant North American predator, the brown bear. And although slightly smaller, this magnificent silver-tipped creature is more ferocious, more unpredictable, and just as omnivorous. Like the polar bear (which is, basically, just a white grizzly) it will eat anything, from plants to people.

In this country we are more familiar with the North American black bear, a vegetarian, and generally shy unless a cub is threatened. But the grizzly is a dangerous, and now endangered, animal. It is quite likely that within the next few decades, it will follow its relative, the Mexican grizzly, into virtual extinction. So although our bears were beyond the age of breeding, they were quite valuable from a number of viewpoints. Our job was to anesthetize them and move them over local streets, expressways, and bridges.

Even the stage directions for our little play, which would soon be splashed across the centerfolds of the New York newspapers, were a problem. The Central Park Zoo had been designed at the turn of the century and was considered a marvel of construction. But the architect had no way of knowing that at some vague time in the future, a handful of men would have to shuttle three eight-hundred-pound bears through its narrow hallways.

All the public ever sees is the outside enclosure, where the pool is. The den, where the bears sleep, is low-ceilinged and covers about the area of an average kitchen. To gain entrance to the den requires going up two small flights of stairs, then down a long, narrow corridor, approximately fifty yards long, poorly lit, and wide enough for two humans (or a single bear) to navigate.

A parks recreational van and an enclosed pickup truck, along with a police car for escort, waited at the exit. Judging the floor areas of the transport vehicles, we found there was only room to move two of the bears on the first trip. The third would have to wait in line for the next bus to Brooklyn.

An official brain trust cued up to plan the move. It included Jim Dooley, an engineer and expert on zoo facilities, the Assistant Parks Commissioner, John Fitzgerald and other zookeepers, and several policemen armed with .38 caliber handguns. Impressive weaponry if you are patrolling Fourty-second Street, but very nearly useless against a creature as large and powerful as a grizzly.

Peering down the cramped corridor, we cursed the long-dead architect. Perhaps bears, like people, were generally smaller three-quarters of a century ago. Or maybe they had moved the bears in as cubs, and they had just grown. Whichever, it was going to be like getting a model ship out of a bottle.

The safest way to proceed would be to anesthetize the bears, crate them up, move them, then give them another injection to wake them up. But they were elderly bears, and I was leery about giving them too strong a preliminary shot of M-99, the anesthetic we were using. The crating and uncrating would take too much time, and the necessity for an extra injection would be almost guaranteed. I had to weigh the safety of the animals against the possible risk to human life. My own included.

M-99 is a very strong, narcotic drug. If you use it on an animal and don't give him the antidote, he's going to die. The antidote, administered intravenously, presents another problem. The animal revives almost instantly. You can easily wind up staring into the eyes of a totally conscious grizzly who is wondering: Why is this person sticking a needle into me? Used on the large herbivores like the rhinoceros, it's a different matter. They are lumbering, slower, and have to get to their feet to attack.

An intravenous shot of M-99 would have been ideal, if I could have walked up to one of the bears, wrapped a strand of rubber around its arm, and said, "Squeeze your fist." But the shot had to be from a tranquilizer gun, intramuscularly, which meant that it would be absorbed at a slower rate. And sometimes the syringes don't go off perfectly, or they bounce away from the animal, and you have no idea whether you have actually injected 8 ccs, 10 ccs, or even 18 ccs. All we could do was take an educated guess at the dosage and hope for the best.

As we debated, I filled several syringes. I had once hit a bear with M-99, then gone into the cage to do some dental work on him. He happened to be stretched out between me and the cage door, and in the middle of the operation he sat up and raised his paw over my head. It's strange how vividly you recall moments like that. It had been raining all day; I was drenched and annoyed to begin with, and my first reaction was to look up at him and tell him to quit being a pest and lie down so I could finish. The dental equipment jutted from his mouth like toothpicks, and his yellow teeth were clotted with blood.

Then I distinctly remember thinking, *I really didn't know I was going to die when I got up this morning.*

The bear got to his feet while I knelt there, knowing that any move I made would only serve to focus his attention on his dentist. I couldn't say whether he was awake or asleep at the time, but he immediately lay back down and closed his eyes. Perhaps he was just having a bad dream. I know I've had several since that encounter.

Two by two, we walked down the hallway and opened a steel door. An inner doorframe, set with steel bars, stood between us and the bears. The male and one of the females were in the den, a few feet from us. The other female was outside, pacing methodically by the pool. Although they were aging bears, it was spring and they were itchy.

Fitzgerald turned a large, creaking wheel that lowered the grill between the outside enclosure and the den. The two isolated bears stirred. As soon as I started firing the tranquilizer gun, they began hurling themselves against the bars, singly at first, then in tandem. The shots echoed loudly in the hallway, and the sudden high cracks didn't improve their dispositions. At the peak of their anger, they were standing side by side, smashing at the bars with their paws.

I was aiming for their legs, reloading in the semidarkness and shooting as fast as possible. Two of the darts misfired, and it was a good forty-five minutes before either of the bears went down. It must have sounded like the gunfight at the O.K. Corral was being restaged in mid-Manhattan.

The tremendous amount of fatty tissue in the leg

muscles slowed the absorption of the anesthetic considerably, and later, when we returned for the third bear, I made sure to shoot for the arm muscles.

Their increased heart rate helped pump the M-99 through their systems, and the force of their blows began to lessen. The female dropped to her forepaws. She lurched against the wall and collapsed. The male redoubled his efforts, eyes blazing with fury. Then his equilibrium faltered. He grabbed at the bars a final time, missed, and dropped.

Although deafened by the shots and chilled by the ferocity of the attack, we swarmed into the den when John opened the inner door. What followed was a routine straight out of the Keystone Cops. Eight of us grabbed the male and converged on the narrow hallway. One supported the monster head, one on each leg, and the others half-dragged the deadweight body. The air was soon filled with muttered curses as knuckles and elbows, backs and buttocks were scraped along the cement walls.

The same routine was repeated with the second bear, the female. She was a bit lighter, six hundred pounds or so, but we managed to scrape and bruise whatever areas of our bodies we had missed on the first passage. The bears were loaded, one in the parks van, the other in the pickup.

As a precaution, Bill Dooley and I went back to the den to make sure none of the tranquilizing darts had been left lying around. We got them all and, as we left, I slammed the inner door behind me. The hinges creaked, then snapped. After three-quarters of an hour of continuous pounding by the bears, metal fatigue and sheer age had destroyed them.

We stood silently for a moment, both envisioning what surely would have happened if the bears had struck it one more time.

"You'd better get that door fixed," I said.

"Next time you want to shuttle some bears around," he said quietly, "count me out."

Dooley is an incredibly dedicated person and has spent many days with me on the Wednesday rounds as we discussed the health and natural habitat of various animals. He does a remarkable job, working within a limited city budget, to upgrade the zoo facilities. But, quite reasonably, he had second thoughts about risking his life.

We split into two groups, manned the vehicles, and pulled out. With any luck, we had about thirty minutes to get the bears into the Prospect Park Zoo before I would have to give them the antidote. The countdown started.

Bill Webster, who had been with me for eleven years and has an almost uncanny feeling for the disposition of animals, joined me in the back of the pickup. We squeezed in around the inert body of the male grizzly. The cab of the truck was packed with officials.

We were halfway to Brooklyn before the bear sat up. I never realized you could fit so many people under a dashboard.

For a moment, it looked like I had grossly underestimated the amount of narcotic that the animal required. But he was still disoriented, and only beginning to elbow his way around when I injected a small shot of the drug. He was sedated quickly, and dropped back into a prone position. Just to be safe, or relatively safe, Bill hog-tied him with heavy rope.

"You ought to get a job in a rodeo," I said.

He smiled, knowing as well as I that even a groggy bear, in the confines of a pickup truck, would be a disaster. I could imagine someone coming in late for work and trying to explain to his boss how he was driving along, right on time, and suddenly a giant grizzly had burst through the side of a passing truck.

A week before the move was scheduled, we had tried to arrange to borrow a couple of paddy wagons from the Police Department. But the bureaucratic lines of communication got fouled up, so the vehicles we used were not exactly bear-proof to start with. After the second injection, however, things went fine until we got to Brooklyn, a spiderweb of angling cross-streets that tend to confuse all but its legendary natives.

I glanced through the window to check our progress. I had driven out to Prospect Park every Wednesday for several years and was quite familiar with the most direct route. My stomach began to sink as a row of unfamiliar street signs flashed by. Whoever had been giving directions to our driver had made a mistake.

The blare of the police siren up ahead made conversation difficult, so I motioned toward the small window with my head and shrugged at Bill. He frowned. If the caravan was delayed very long, another shot of M-99 would be necessary—and probably fatal—for the bear.

We had no idea, of course, how the bear in the other van was holding up. We learned, later, that she had slept peacefully throughout the trip. It was sheer luck. M-99, even though it seemed to work well on a variety of species, was still a relatively new anesthetic. And, as always, there was the uncertainty as to the exact physiological status of a particular animal's detoxification mechanisms.

It always amazes me to watch them anesthetize large animals on the popular wildlife television shows. They always seem to administer the perfect dose, the animal always drops, and there is never any trouble with the antidote. What you don't see are the animals that crash off into the bush and don't survive, or the ones that need a second shot, or the ones that wake up a little too fast. Film editors, I suppose, have to keep in mind the fact that most of these shows are scheduled for after-dinner viewing.

I knocked on the front window. The driver nodded hastily, already aware that we were off course. Everyone in the cab seemed to be talking at the same time. We began to zigzag, looking for Flatbush Avenue, which leads directly to the park. Minutes dragged by. I kept hoping that the police car leading us would pull over and ask a native how to get to the zoo.

We felt the truck shift into high as it wheeled around a corner and knew the driver must have located Flatbush. Within minutes, we roared into Prospect Park with all the subtlety of an armored tank attack.

Mid-afternoon strollers scattered as we poured out of the trucks. Being of a more modern design than Central Park, the Prospect bear den was easily accessible—no narrow, endless corridors to deal with. Hastily, we manhandled the sedated animals into the safety of their new home. I injected the antidote shots into both of them and they regained consciousness—dazed at first, then lapsing into their usual ill humor while they explored the unfamiliar den.

Our battered crew assembled outside the bear enclosure, while various cuts and scrapes were treated. By mutual consent, we decided to wait until the next day to move the final grizzly.

With a slightly larger dose of M-99, she passed out more rapidly than the others had, and there was no trouble during the move. I was confident that when it came time to return them to Central Park, we would have smooth sailing. It is a fallacy to count your bears before they're caged.

When the pool had been drained and repaired, John Fitzgerald and I met with Mr. Kinzig of the Prospect Zoo to plan the return of the bad news bears.

The mid-afternoon traffic, we agreed, had been a little heavier than expected on the first trip. I suggested we try it in the early morning. Kinzig thought five o'clock would be a good time, but John said four would be even better.

Being a night person by habit, I knew the only conceivable way I could do anything at four in the morning would be to stay up all night, and I really didn't want to move grizzlies without sufficient sleep. We settled on five, which would give us plenty of time to beat the morning rush hour.

I met Dr. Woods in front of the office well before sunup, and we were joined by several volunteers—student vets who were anxious to gain practical experience in handling large animals. They were full of excitement and anticipation, convinced that the venture would be fun. I often feel the same way, but rarely at that hour. We pulled into Prospect Park at exactly five o'clock.

Fitzgerald was already there with the police escort. We shuffled around in the predawn darkness, sipping from containers of coffee. Dr. Woods began filling syringes while our assistants went off to check on the bears. They were awake, they reported, and as content as grizzlies ever get.

Kinzig arrived shortly with the first item of bad news. There had been a mixup between park and police officials. The policemen who were there to escort us were scheduled to go off duty within the hour.

We hurried to the administration building, opened the switchboard, and started calling officials. It was nearly 5:30. No one could be reached who could sanction an extension of the policemen's shift. And about the last thing we needed was to drive through half of Manhattan without an escort.

The chief of police was out of town. The parks commissioner wasn't in yet. The mayor was at a convention. We got a busy signal on the governor's hotline. As we neared the end of our list of official sanctioners, the policemen themselves got together and talked it over. They decided to stick with us, unauthorized and without pay, until the job was done. It wasn't the world's most enticing assignment, especially for the officer who would be riding shotgun with us, but they were extremely cooperative and understanding.

From outside the enclosure we lured two of the bears to a narrow section and penned them there to restrict movement. The third refused to fall for any offers of food or companionship. She had evidently taken a liking to

Brooklyn and was in no mood to travel. We came to the conclusion that Prospect Park really needed a grizzly, and Kinsig was delighted. We had a larger parks van this time, one that would accomodate two bears. Only one trip would be necessary.

Because I had more room to move around and place my shots, the bears succumbed with a minimum of earth-shaking roars. Loading them seemed like a piece of cake, even though the cake weighed nearly eight hundred pounds. Dr. Woods monitored one bear with a stethoscope, a syringe full of antidote and another syringe full of M-99 handy. I did the same with the other.

The last person to climb into the back of the van was a policeman from the special tactical squad carrying a shotgun. He was very calm and matter of fact, obviously not the type who would use a weapon unless there was a drastic emergency. Assuming that their systems would stand the drugs, we felt the bears would sleep throughout the trip. But if one of them awoke, and we couldn't sedate it quickly enough, he would have to open fire. At that range, one shot would probably take out both the bears, plus the people, the van, and about half a block of downtown Brooklyn.

Flatbush Avenue was nearly deserted when we pulled out. The screaming police car was in the lead, then the parks van, followed closely by my own car. I had traded the skunk-smelling Rolls in on a dark blue Ferrari—which I almost had to leave in Prospect Park. I think New York has the highest percentage of nondrivers in any city in America. I'm not sure whether that's a tribute to the efficiency of the Metropolitan Transit Authority, or an indication of the scarcity of parking spaces. Just before we left, I asked if anyone would volunteer to drive my car into Manhattan, behind the procession. Out of the dozen people present, I found only four who knew how to drive, and none of them had ever driven a stickshift car. I had to enlist the aid of a parks chauffeur who had come into work early.

We bullied our way through the gradually increasing traffic. We got some odd looks from the drivers who pulled over to let us pass. Motorcades are usually reserved for visiting dignitaries in limousines.

By the time we had crossed the Manhattan Bridge and turned onto F.D.R. Drive, it began to look like we'd make it with no trouble. Then the bear I was monitoring stopped breathing.

Dr. Woods must have seen me tense up. We both looked at the syringe full of antidote, then at the shotgun in the policeman's hands. There was no time to rehash alternatives. Quickly, I injected 2 ccs, hoping it would be enough to revive breathing, but not enough to wake him up.

The special forces officer sat there, stony cool, quite aware of what could easily happen in the next few seconds. I concentrated on the stethoscope, trying to block everything else from my mind.

The bear's heart fluttered. He gasped, then exhaled. The jaws opened. He labored. Another gasp. I nodded to Dr. Woods. A regular pattern returned as his breathing slowed and steadied. He was alive and asleep. We relaxed.

We turned west on Fifty-seventh Street and three minutes later were in Central Park. I heard our driver ask someone, "What the hell's going on?" The reply was drowned out by the squeal of brakes as we came to a halt.

The back door of the van flew open and we jumped out, blinking in the sunlight. We hadn't expected a reception committee; the shuttling about of dangerous predators is not as well publicized as the arrival of movie stars. But, within fifty yards of us, there was a mob.

Park administrators, press photographers, and groups of curious citizens were walking toward our vehicles. In the confusion, we learned that some sort of early morning dedication ceremony was scheduled in front of the next building, and the photographers obviously thought we were part of that event.

Police officers from our escort car, aided by park workers, formed a line between the van and the entrance to the bear den. The female was closest to the rear of the van, so we eased her out first. Once she came into view, the crowd began to grow. People deserted the ceremony site in droves.

Everyone seemed to have suggestions about the best way to carry a sleeping bear. Children fought to get through the police line for a better view. A circus atmosphere prevailed. Among the onlookers, anyway.

The van was closed and we trundled the female into the corridor leading to the den. It was comforting to see that they had replaced the doorframe that had been so badly battered weeks before.

We returned to the van, discussing how we could get the larger male grizzly through the hallway without suffering another bout of bruises and cuts. He took care of the problem for us.

I was standing a few feet from Fitzgerald when he opened the van. Suddenly he was backing toward me, and I threw up my hands to avoid a collision. The small amount of antidote I had given the bear had been totally absorbed and had worked too well. The bear rolled out of the van and stood up in the middle of Central Park.

There was a panic.

Some of the officials must have remembered that they had urgent letters to dictate. They fled. Women plucked their children from the front lines and headed for parts unknown. Flashbulbs turned the scene incandescent as the normally fearless photographers fired away, back-pedalling all the while.

The policemen, relieved of the duty of holding back a curious crowd, turned toward us and began to draw their weapons. The grizzly was not fully awake, but even in a dazed condition he towered fearsomely over his rapidly disappearing audience.

It had all happened so quickly that my only thought was for the safety of the bear. "It's okay," I yelled at the policemen, "everything's under control! Don't shoot!"

They didn't look very convinced. I don't imagine I sounded very convincing.

Several zookeepers moved forward and surrounded him. The groggy beast stumbled and staggered a few feet. The circle widened and they kept just out of his reach. He regained his balance and began to take note of his environs.

Expecting to hear a volley of shots at any moment, I raced for the van and grabbed a syringe of M-99. The shouts and screams of the retreating mob only served to make him more alert.

My hands were trembling as I entered the circle of zookeepers, slightly on his flank. He had lowered his arms and was standing motionless, getting his bearings. I jabbed.

The bear huffed as the needle went in. He turned toward me. His eyes began to glaze, and within moments he was off in another world—one inhabited by his ancestors, perhaps, where there were no cages and no scuttling little bipeds to annoy him.

"Is he out?" asked Fitzgerald.

"I think so," I said, "but he probably won't go down for another couple minutes."

"Maybe we can get him to walk."

"Worth a try," I said. If it worked, it would certainly shorten the time the bear would have to spend under the second full dose of anesthetic and would enhance his chances of surviving it.

The volunteer assistants, zookeepers, Dr. Woods, John, and myself—ten of us in all, started pushing and pulling him in the general direction of his den. Like a giant reluctant dog, he moved. Up the stairs, then into the hallway. His musky odor filled the air. I had visions of him collapsing and falling on those of us who were crawling over each other to push from behind.

Because of our slow progress, the journey seemed endless. Several times he stopped and staggered backwards before we could shift his momentum. Eventually someone up ahead broke away and we heard the cage door opening. With a final shove, we sent him weaving into the den.

The female was curled in the corner, dead to the world. But the male, securely back in his own familiar territory, turned to face us again. Dr. Woods left immediately and was soon back with syringes of antidote.

"Let's bring them around," I said.

Fitzgerald and I stepped into the den. We edged around to the female and injected her. Then John walked boldly up to the male and waved his hands in front of its face. I approached from the rear and emptied the syringe into it. Without waiting for a reaction, we exited.

Two of the grizzlies are now living in Central Park with a pool drainage system, which we hope will function for many years to come. The third, a loner by nature, seems quite content in Brooklyn. There are no plans in the works for ever moving any of them again.

The spectacular photographs of a grizzly loose in Central Park made all the local papers. Reading the stories, I realized how exciting the lives of people who deal with such animals must seem. There is rarely any notice of the hard work and drudgery that goes into the maintenance of a zoo and the care of its animals.

With no time to celebrate our success, the zoo attendants went back to their regular jobs, the policemen finally went off duty, and I wound up late for my office hours.

Two of my clients wanted to know why they had to be kept waiting, after making early appointments. After all, if they could show up on time, didn't I have the courtesy to do the same?

I apologized, treated their pets, and said I'd try to see that I wasn't late next time.

8

Barnaby and Other Stars of Stage, Screen, and Dog Food Commercials

The star syndrome is a virtually incurable disease. People tend to think of it in conjunction with those few rare movie or television personalities who like to throw the weight of their fame around, once they've reached the upper strata of their profession. This overinflation of the ego can also affect animals—or at least it seemed that way to those of us who lived and worked with Barnaby, our resident movie star.

Throughout his career, from the sheep dog in numerous television commercials to his starring role in *Serpico* with Al Pacino, he maintained the animal equivalent of a sense of humor. But I suppose I would begin to feel a bit pampered (and sometimes petulant) if I were a dog and found myself being picked up by a limousine and driven to work every morning.

Living in Manhattan, I've had the chance to treat a good many show business animals and the personal pets of a number of stars. Jane Powell, Barbra Streisand, Dick Cavett, and Joel Grey visit the office from time to time and have all taken an active interest in wildlife conservation. Ms. Streisand is very dedicated to her dog, a poodle, and once called from the West Coast, where she was making a film. Her dog, it seems, was showing all the signs of being pregnant. The problem was that it had not, to her knowledge, been bred. She asked if I could fly out to the coast to examine the dog, as she wouldn't be returning to New York for several months, when shooting on the film was completed. I was sorely tempted to abandon the eastern winter for a few days of sunshine, but I was impossibly busy. I recommended a Los Angeles vet whose work I was familiar with and asked her to let me know how things turned out.

A few weeks went by, during which time Caroline came to work for me. She was an immediate, steadying influence on the Milts' menagerie and took on the jobs of receptionist, secretary, appointment scheduler, and check-writer-outer. Nearly unflappable, no matter what sort of odd creature was trotted into the waiting room. Then she called me up to the front one afternoon, her eyes wide with wonder. She handed me the phone and said, "I think it's Barbra Streisand."

I nodded, took the phone, chatted for a few minutes, laughed, then hung up.

"Was that . . . ?"

"Yeah. Her dog had a false pregnancy."

Although I was the vet for the Dawn Animal Agency (run by the Brooks, to help support the less fortunate animals on their farm), it never occurred to me to try casting any of our office pets in commercials. But in 1974, we heard that another small ad agency was looking for a calm, cool, and collected cat for a rather frenetic commercial. Who, we realized, would be more qualified for the job than Arnold? He was totally blind, so the lights on the set wouldn't bother him at all. And he was more sure-footed than any animal I'd ever met. The noise wouldn't bother him, either. As a permanent fixture in the office, he was used to a constant din. And he was docile. An occasional scratch behind the ears kept him happy for hours on end.

There are regulations, however, that cover the use of animals with disabilities in filming. I know of a horse, for instance, who was so well trained and perfect for a commercial that he was hired despite the fact that he limped badly. For the concluding scene, he was shot full of cortisone to make him run faster. The regulations against such measures are necessary to help control cruelty to animals but, knowing Arnold, we thought he would be great. And someone from the office would be on the scene at all times. Florence, my wife (from whom I am separated), carried him down to the tryouts.

Florence is one of my best friends: a sensible, level-headed woman who has successfully run several businesses, while raising funds for needy causes. She breezed in, signed up for Arnold's screen test, and didn't mention that he was blind. Barbara Austin, the agency representative, was with her, just to show her the ropes and introduce her to the director.

The small, brightly-lit studio was chaotic. Technicians and cameramen bustled around, making adjustments for each take. Professional animal handlers were there, looking to rent their wares, and a good many stage mothers, seeking fame for their pet tabbies. In the center of the room was an ornate table, set lavishly with silverware, candelabra, champagne, and—as a centerpiece—a gleaming bowl heaped with the sponsor's product. Cat food.

Arnold ignored the growling, hissing multitude around him, and when Florence carried him over and sat him down on the table, he began to eat the cat food with just the proper amount of feline dignity they were looking for. Florence grinned and nudged Barbara, barely able to contain her excitement.

But the commercial was to be shot in color, and Arnold's basic gray coloration, among all that silver, struck the director as being wrong.

"Sorry, but that cat just doesn't read well," he said, meaning there was trouble in the color definition.

"How could you tell he was blind!" shouted Florence.

Barbara grabbed her by the arm.

"What?" asked the director.

"Nothing," said Barbara, scooping up Arnold and pushing an irate Florence toward the door, "She's just upset because her cat didn't get the commercial!"

On the way back to the office, Barbara explained some of the technical terms used by people in the television industry. Arnold's career was nipped in the bud. He went back to being just plain blind Arnold.

The basic plot for *A Star Is Born* has just about been done to death by Hollywood. But one of the reasons that this old rags-to-riches story is still so popular is that from time to time it still occurs in real life. I can testify to that, because it happened to a fuzzy little crossbreed mutt I met named "Toto, too".

One of my Murray Hill neighbors was leaving town. He was going to be on the road for an extended time and asked us to help find a home for his dog. Rather than dragging it from city to city or boarding it indefinitely, he felt it would be better off with a new owner.

I agreed. He brought it in, I checked it over, then called the Brook farm. "Leonard," I said, "do you know anyone who might want a feisty little bright-eyed dog?"

"What breed?"

"American."

"I see. No papers, right?"

"Nothing the Kennel Club would recognize," I said, "he's a little terrier, a little beagle, a little Great Dane, a little . . ."

"You're in luck. Some people called the other day, looking for that exact mixture. I have to come into town tonight anyway, so could you have him ready?"

"Right. And I'll forge a passport for him so he can get into New Jersey."

"Very funny. Has he had his shots and everything?"

"Yes, he's in good physical shape. I'll see you later."

He picked up the dog shortly after six o'clock, then drove across town to the Broadway Theater on Fifty-third Street, where the hit musical *The Wiz* was playing. One of the Brooks' dogs was appearing as Toto in this stage version of *The Wizard of Oz*, and Len had to see the handler on business. It's a long show and consequently has a 7:30 curtain instead of the traditional eight o'clock opening. Len arrived at 6:45, went backstage, and left the mutt in a carrier with the stage manager.

The handler rushed up to him and said, "Toto dropped dead."

Len was shocked. The little dog that they had trained so carefully for the role had just recently been checked over. But even dogs in perfect health are not immune to a heart attack or stroke.

Hundreds of people were already filling the theater, expecting to spend an evening with Dorothy, the Cowardly Lion, the Tin Woodsman, and, of course, Toto.

The director approached them and asked, "Where's Toto?"

"We're having a substitute tonight," said Len, "the stage manager has him." He turned to the handler. "You want to go get him?"

It was the handler's turn to look shocked. But he hustled off to get the dog.

The evening performance of *The Wiz* opened with Len, holding the new Toto, crouched just offstage. The handler stood in the wings at the other side of the stage, ready to catch the dog if he decided to take an unscheduled exit.

On cue Len released him. The dog trotted out on stage and began to frolic with Dorothy, completely unabashed by the presence of the orchestra or audience.

The dog performed faultlessly. He charmed the entire cast, the unsuspecting audience, and the greatly relieved Leonard Brook.

The angry-looking director approached him after the final curtain call. "Len," he said, "why didn't you bring this dog in in the first place? He's great!"

The dog is still appearing nightly in the show. The cast calls him Toto, Too.

You can never be completely sure how an animal is going to react on stage. No matter how obedience trained it is, animal handlers live with the constant fear of disaster.

Mozart never wrote any horse operas, but several of the animals were used in a recent production of *The Marriage of Figaro*. A friend of mine is a bassoonist with the orchestra at the New York City Opera. She's an accomplished musician and has learned to play with one eye on the conductor and the other on the stage.

One evening, in the middle of the show, the horses got panicky. My friend saw the conductor swing his baton up, and suddenly an expression of sheer horror crossed his face. Someone, my friend thought, must have hit an awfully sour note. She glanced to her right and saw several musicians pressed up against the wall, under the stage apron. Still playing their instruments, of course. And directly above her two wild horses were thundering toward the edge of the stage, seemingly intent on making their exit via the orchestra pit.

The horses reared, and came to a halt. Most of the audience must have thought it was part of the show, as there were only a few scattered gasps. I'm sure many people marveled that horses could be trained that precisely.

If putting animals on stage can be frightening, putting them on film can be frustrating. Barnaby certainly caused his share of headaches for the directors he worked with. And much like Toto, Too, he started his show business career as a stand-in.

Patrick was Barbara Austin's superstar sheep dog. For a period of five or six years, whenever a sheep dog was needed for a television commercial, most people in the industry automatically called for Patrick. He could practically read a script.

On July 4, 1972 he came down with acute gastric dilatation, which is fatal virtually all of the time. The stomach gets twisted, fills up with gas, and the victim is dead within the hour. Even if an immediate operation is performed, the animal often dies from the anesthetic or from shock.

Patrick was old—twelve or so. The smaller breeds usually have a longer life expectancy. A fifteen-year-old Chihuahua isn't rare at all. A fifteen-year-old sheep dog is nearly unheard of. Barnaby died in 1978 at the age of thirteen—the equivalent of a man in his late eighties.

Barbara Austin, Patrick's trainer and owner, rushed him to my office as soon as the dilatation started. The pain must have been terrible. He was snapping and foaming at the mouth; it was all Bill Webster and I could do to hold him down while the anesthetic took effect. The surgery lasted for four hours. Patrick survived it and was retired.

He had been scheduled to film a new commercial a few days later, and a replacement had to be found. There sat Barnaby, descended from champions, registered with the Kennel Club, and winner of numerous obedience school awards. He responded to commands beautifully. If he was in the right mood.

Barbara took him out for a walk to put him through his paces. He must have been in the mood to show off, for she returned to the office convinced that she had found the perfect replacement for Patrick. We warned her that, when Florence took him out, he would often head for parts unknown, dragging her reluctantly along on the other end of the leash. Barbara was sure she could handle him.

Sheep dogs (or, as they are officially classified, old English sheep dogs) rarely win prizes in canine competitions. One will jump a fence gracefully and return to heel. Everyone applauds, so naturally, the dog does it again. The audience loves it, but dog show judges frown on such freelance frolics. The breed seems cursed with both a need for approval and a sense of humor.

Barnaby was utterly delighted to be in the spotlight at that first filming. He ignored Barbara's every command, wolfed down the dog food, and attempted to make friends with everyone on the set.

The director finally exploded, and asked Barbara, in no uncertain terms, to kindly remove that heathen creature from the premises. But the sponsor—obviously a fine judge of canine character—was there and recognized a certain *joie de vivre* in Barnaby that appealed to him.

"I like this dog," he said. "I want this dog in my commercial. Rewrite the damn script, and do whatever the dog is doing."

The cameramen were upset. The director was

enraged. And the writers were stuck with having to come up with a whole new commercial.

The final product—which amounted to thirty seconds of Barnaby chasing an animated prairie schooner across a slippery kitchen floor—was a big success.

Barbara related the story and suffered through a good many I-told-you-so nods. Then she started looking for a different sheep dog to replace Patrick. Fate was against her. She called shortly after the ad was seen on national television.

"We're on a roll," she said, "Barnaby's got another job."

"I thought you were—"

"They requested him. Specifically."

One of the cameramen on the set had worked on Barnaby's first commercial and recognized him as soon as he trotted in. Word spread among the technicians: this is going to be a toughie.

The inevitable bowl of dog food was, this time, sitting on a beautiful white rug. The first thing Barnaby did was to walk to the middle of the rug, directly in front of the camera, then crouch, and deliver a perfectly normal stool.

He looked around for the expected approval but was met by a shocked silence. Barbara, lacking a handy window to jump out of, merely groaned.

This particular director, being on a tight shooting schedule, displayed a good deal of patience. He decided to replace the rug rather than the dog and hope for the best. And just to show them, Barnaby went through the whole thing letter perfect.

"I must be out of my mind," Barbara said, as she came by to collect Barnaby for yet another job. The ninety-pound, shaggy dog ambled up to her, his stump of a tail bobbing with delight.

"If he acts up again," I said, "drag him off the set and threaten him. He probably figures you're bluffing when you give him commands. You've got to lay it on the line."

They went, he goofed off, and she dragged him into a corner. In a very harsh tone Barbara threatened to blacken both his eyes, shave him bald, and throw what was left to her pet tiger. Properly cowed, Barnaby trotted through two takes as though they were child's play. (There was, in fact, a child involved in the ad.) The shooting was finished before lunch, and the jubilant director came over to lavish praise on both Barbara and Barnaby. "Wow!" he exclaimed, "Can you believe it? This dog is terrific!"

Barbara smiled and patted the dog, who stood at heel beside her. She listened politely as the director continued. After all, it was a matter of money and good will for the agency, and possible future employment for Barnaby. Then she felt something warm trickling down the inside of one of her boots. Her smile hardened a bit, but otherwise there was no indication of what was happening. When the director finished, she turned and sloshed out of the building.

Barnaby followed at her heels, a look of divine innocence on his face.

For some unknown reason, Barbara decided not to go along when Barnaby got an on-location job in Virginia. She sent an assistant with him, even though the assignment looked easy. They needed some footage of a large dog helping a farmer round up some sheep and cattle.

Sheep dogs have a natural tendency to herd things. The ones used on real farms are trained intensively, but it is instinctive in all of them. Barnaby used to practice on the office cats, and occasionally on the clients in the waiting room.

The crew checked into a Holiday Inn near the farm where they would be filming. The area was beautiful: low, rolling green pastures—the perfect spot for filming a commercial to convince people that, after a hard day's work, farmers find time to sit down with a glass of the sponsor's beer.

Barnaby was fed and placed in the kennel behind the inn, and the crew retired for the night. Barnaby was a city dog. He had never slept anywhere other than in a house, with people.

The next morning, he was discovered, peacefully sleeping in the main lobby. Like any civilized person.

The assistant called Barbara, who called me for advice.

"Get him a room," I said. "One with an air-conditioner. He likes fresh air."

They got him a room. With an air-conditioner. And a balcony.

On location, Barnaby was presented with fifteen grazing cows and was commanded to herd them toward a corner of the pasture. It was duck soup—or at least beef bouillon—for an animal with his instincts. He was released; he swept around the herd, barking and snapping with authority. They moved in the right direction, as the camera captured the action. Barnaby dashed madly back and forth, snapping at the heels of stragglers. They went through the scene three times, and his enthusiasm never slackened.

It rained that night, but the weather cleared early the next morning. They wanted to film the same scene, substituting sheep for cows. The sheep dog is a breed that dates back to the early eighteenth century. It was developed in England, and used to help herd sheep to market. Barnaby, the crew agreed, would have no trouble. This kind of work was in his blood. Driving out to the farm, they began to think about wrapping things up by noon.

The cameras were started up, Barnaby was released, and he thundered toward the herd. Ten yards from them, he came to a dead halt. His nose quivered. He turned, trotted complacently back to the side of his handler, and sat down.

They dragged him toward the sheep. He shrank back and wouldn't even look at the creatures. The handler was at a loss to explain Barnaby's reluctance. Then he took a whiff of the air near the herd.

Sheep live out-of-doors the year round. Their heavy wool protects them in the winter, and they are sheared in the spring. Between times, they are rarely washed. The rain of the previous night and the warm morning sun had combined to produce an odor that even a sheep dog found offensive. At least, this particular sheep dog.

They tried everything they could think of to get him interested in the herd, including the liberal use of spray deodorants. He was having none of it. That segment of the script was discarded. But in the final analysis, all the commercials he had done turned out, on screen, highly successful. He began to get the reputation of being a well-trained, talented—and sensitive—actor.

When he hit the big time, Barnaby's true colors began to show. *Serpico* was basically a serious movie, and Barnaby seemed to have a natural inclination toward comedy. He was chosen for the role of Serpico's beloved pet, nonetheless. Barbara Austin took on the job of handling him, even though she sensed impending disaster.

They began filming the movie, which starred Al Pacino as a corruption-fighting detective, in New York in August. Naturally, one of the first scenes scheduled was supposed to take place in the dead of winter.

A street near the west side waterfront was closed to traffic, wind and snow machines were set up off-camera, and the cast members sweated under heavy coats and boots. The temperature was in the upper nineties.

Sheep dogs are cold weather animals, bred to feel right at home in the harsh northern climates. Barnaby was suffering but dutifully lumbered along at Barbara's side toward the location. Suddenly he looked up and recognized his kind of weather, a hundred yards away.

They were in the middle of filming a tense dramatic scene when a mammoth black and white snowball erupted among them, scattering carefully arranged fake snowdrifts in every direction.

A number of takes were required to finish the scene. The cast kept breaking up.

After his explosive introduction to film (which ended up, of course, on the cutting room floor) Barnaby soon made friends with Sidney Lumet, the director, and with Al Pacino. During the shooting of interiors, he sat patiently beside Mr. Lumet's chair and was so well behaved that they didn't bother keeping a leash on him. Their faith in him was justified, and he only interrupted one other scene.

In the scene, Al Pacino got shot. He keeled over, as a camera moved in for a close-up on his face. Barnaby, seeing his friend in obvious torment, trotted over to nuzzle him and offer condolences. Pacino giggled.

There was no trouble finding work for Barnaby after *Serpico* was released. All Barbara had to do was mention that he was the dog in it. Barnaby was a star and was treated as such. He would frolic through a scene, and the director would say, "You know, maybe the dog's got something." Then they would rewrite to work the commercial around his antics.

They were right. He did have something. It's called the star syndrome.

9

The Glades

Most of my work involves the treatment of captive animals. It is satisfying in many ways. But occasionally I feel the need to observe them where they belong, in the wilds. And when this itch, this desire to escape from the boundaries of civilization that encircle both myself and the zoo animals, becomes unbearable, I find myself returning like a migratory bird to Flamingo.

Flamingo is a remote village at the southern end of the Florida Everglades. It is little more than a marina and a camping supply store, perched on the edge of what is probably the most desolate area in continental America. The great white bird for which the village was named has disappeared from the cape, wiped out by poachers when flamingo feathers became fashionable.

I am naturally drawn to the wilderness and fell in love with the Glades on a brief trip to Florida in 1960. The stunted growth, the marine life, the incredible balance of nature that exists in this 4,000 square-mile-fresh-water-saltwater marsh has brought me back again and again. Flamingo, an outpost run by the national park rangers, has become my usual jumping-off place for personal exploration.

I have always tried to avoid guided tours and one-day excursions into wilderness areas. There is just no way to get the unique feel for a region while sitting on a crowded bus or following a guide down well-worn paths. Understanding the varieties of life in a wilderness takes time, patience, and solitude. The rewards, I think, are enormous, and the dangers involved can be minimized by proper preparation. Usually.

Survival gear, as important as a knowledge of one's own physical limitations, is dictated by the environment to be faced. On my first extensive trip to the Everglades, I took along what turned out to be the absolute essentials: a compass, proper clothing, and a corned beef sandwich.

Ruth, my first wife, was with me. She had recently completed a course in oceanography at the Museum of Natural History, and we were anxious to explore the wild regions along Florida's western coast. Cape Sable seemed an ideal target to start. It can only be reached by boat, and although an occasional guided tour stops there, we wanted to see it on our own.

We rented a skiff with an outboard motor at the marina and were told it would take about forty minutes to reach Cape Sable. The water looked a little choppy on

Florida Bay, but we were confident. It's a very wide, very shallow bay, extending from the Keys to the Gulf of Mexico. It must cover a thousand square miles and, because of its depth and location, is one of the most fertile breeding grounds of life in the entire world.

We learned later that, only moments after we cleared Flamingo Harbor, the Coast Guard had hoisted small craft warnings. Hurricanes normally take four to eight days to develop, but the winds that sweep around the southern tip of Florida are highly variable and can change drastically in a matter of minutes.

With a steadily increasing wind behind us, we reached Cape Sable within twenty minutes. Naturally, we didn't recognize it.

"I think we're heading up into the Gulf," Ruth said, "look at the waves."

They were coming in long straight rows, broadsiding us, and growing larger. "We've only been out half an hour," I said, "let's stick with it. Shouldn't be long."

The first of a series of large waves caught us, drenching our picnic lunch. We decided it would be prudent to head in. With some previous boating experience, we were both aware of the limitations of a sixteen-foot skiff in rough waters. Turning toward the shore, we sloughed through the rising tide and approached a beach.

I went over the side to prop up the motor, while Ruth splashed to the shore. The proping mechanism, a simple set of bars that swing down under the motor and keep the blades from becoming embedded in the sand, was faulty. I dragged the skiff in as far as possible, until the bow seemed secure, then waded in.

The beach was dazzling. A showcase of brilliant,

multicolored shells seemed to stretch unbroken along the shore to the very rim of the world. Because of its pristine state, this area had obviously never been visited by commercial tours, or even the collectors who ranged the beaches gathering shells to polish and sell to tourists. Odd, we thought, for Cape Sable. We were, of course, many miles to the north—and lost, for all intents and purposes.

Luckily, we weren't aware of that. Had we known, and started back toward Flamingo any sooner, we would have hit the storm that followed us up the Gulf.

We explored, never getting more than a mile or so from the beach, where the Tahiti-like setting gradually changed into the ecology of the great swamp. When it began to rain, we returned to the beach and huddled under a tree.

Clouds tumbled in, moving up the Gulf. There were no boats, large or small, within sight. It occurred to me that we might have some difficulty getting back to Flamingo. We had a slightly oversized rowboat equipped with an outboard motor and would be facing a stiff headwind on a choppy sea. We sat with an eye on the skiff, fearing it might be pulled loose by the tide, leaving us stranded. It was anchored, much too securely, in the mud.

The clouds began to break apart, and brilliant shafts of sunlight illuminated the southern horizon. When the water beyond the breakers looked calm enough, we decided to venture out. Neither of us noticed the sleek gray body that had drifted in just below the surface.

Ruth gathered our things together while I waded out to the boat. Standing armpit-deep in the rolling water,

I concentrated on tearing away the weeds that had collected around the motor blades.

Something struck me from behind, and I was suddenly tumbling to the bottom, the surf surging around me. There was no time for wondering what had happened. I got my feet squared beneath me and pushed up.

I emerged, shocked, sputtering, and cursing what I thought was the undertow. It took me several seconds to recognize the sound I was hearing. It was Ruth, screaming. She was frozen, approximately thirty yards from me, pointing to my right. I looked over. A large fin cut through the breakers, moving in a steady arc that would lead it back to me.

By the time a great white shark reaches a length of four feet, it is considered dangerous to man. This one was about half-grown, perhaps a yard shorter than our sixteen-foot skiff. Books and movies like *Jaws* have alerted the public to the dangers of this voracious predator, but there is no real way to communicate the horror that grips a potential victim.

The fin seemed to pause at the top of its arc. Then it turned toward me and speeded up.

Without thinking, I reached up, grasped the edge of the boat with both hands, and vaulted completely over it. Later, Ruth said I came out of the water like an exploding rocket, and when I tried to duplicate the feat, the best I could do was to struggle up into the skiff.

I scrambled into the boat as the shark passed. For an instant it was stretched at full length beside me, its nose tilted up, mouth gaping open. As it turned, the crescent shaped tail struck the boat and sent it rocking wildly. Then it was gone, retracing the circle for a third pass. I was sure that this time he would come up into the boat after me. A great white, even a half-grown one, could easily turn our small skiff into driftwood.

Quickly I looked around for something to fight him off with. An oar, or anything that might distract his attention. There was nothing—except a waterlogged corned beef sandwich, left over from our lunch.

I snatched it up, and as the shark turned toward me for another run, I tossed the sandwich into its path. The sandwich disappeared like an undersized jellybean in the mouth of a child. The shark wavered, then abruptly turned out to sea. Fifty yards beyond me, it began to glide back and forth, patroling the shoreline. It had swallowed the appetizer and was awaiting the main course.

When I considered it to be far enough off, I leaped out of the boat and hastily splashed to the beach and collapsed. Ruth was as shaken as I was.

Nearly an hour passed before the shark lost interest and moved on, and we were settled enough to free the boat. Great whites are not often seen so close to shore in the Gulf of Mexico, but the strong currents caused by the storm had probably driven it in. The trip back to Flamingo seemed to take hours. Neither of us mentioned the possibility of meeting the shark in open water, but we both watched the rippling surface carefully.

I have been to the Glades on ten separate occasions, and each time, my fascination for the area grows. Every few years there is a frost, which kills just enough plants to keep it from becoming a pure jungle. It is not a forest, because the tremendous flow of water from Lake Okeechobee to the north makes it basically a river of grass. A river with an average depth of two inches. In the rainy season, of course, you can step off a trail into thigh-deep water, but the average depth is less than that of the New York gutters during a healthy rainstorm.

As you travel south from the top of the Glades, which used to reach many miles north of Miami, the salinity of the water changes, as do the types of grass, trees, insects, birds, and mammals. It's a very unique and fragile environment.

Periodic fires clear the hardwood trees and much of the brush away, leaving the evergreens. The Glades is probably the only place in the world that has an evergreen that sheds its leaves for the winter season, and a deciduous tree that keeps its leaves twelve months a year.

Mosquitoes abound during the summer months; they seem to swarm in low areas. I've seen hikers coming back to camp looking like they'd been assaulted with whips. Head nets and insect repellant are necessities for any extensive exploring. Microlife feeds on the mosquito larvae, and some fish feed on the plankton and algae. Small birds eat the bigger fish, alligators, cats, and other animals feed on the fish and birds, and when they die they decompose and fertilize the soil. If the chain of life were interrupted and the Glades were sprayed to wipe out the mosquitoes, it would be a dead area within two years.

Basically, the Everglades are flat. A hummock that reaches three feet above sea level is considered a mountain. There are three species of mangrove tree, and in many places the grass is saw-toothed and so sharp that hiking with shorts on is impossible.

With the great land boom in Florida, the Glades were being destroyed. Half a million acres were reclaimed for agricultural use, and they began building canals east-west across the state which blocked the entire supply of fresh water. When I was there a few years ago, it was so arid that an estimated ninety percent of all the waterfowl had simply vanished. It was obvious that another decade of man's intrusion would wipe out this natural wonder.

Drastically altering the water supply was not the only problem. Many first-time visitors to the Glades are stunned by the vast number of brown pelicans in the area, but as I returned again and again, I realized their numbers were shrinking steadily. The enemy was DDT.

As the algae and plankton absorbed this spray, the concentration of it grew as it moved up the food chain from smaller to larger fish. The brown pelican eats large fish. The dose with every bite was not enough to kill it but was large enough to change gradually the calcium metabolism. That resulted in very thin-skinned, fragile eggs. So all the eggs were being broken merely by the pressure of this bird—which is not exactly a slender, delicate creature—sitting on them during the hatching period. As recently as five years ago, ecologists and ornithologists with an eye to the future considered the brown pelican to be biologically extinct.

Fortunately, members of the Congress and George Hickle, Secretary of the Interior at the time, helped push through legislation to control both the water blockage and the use of DDT. The snowballing deterioration of the Glades has slowed and a gradual reversal is hoped for. But it was reaching the point of no return, and all for the sake of a few more farms, a few more suburban developments, a few more condominiums.

During recent years, some of the trails have been widened enough to allow motoring into the Glades. You can reach a fairly remote area, park the car, and hike on from there. Some of the trails wind near clearings where the wildlife watcher can, with luck, spot a rare species. And occasionally, something that just isn't supposed to exist.

One morning I was driving alone, heading for where I knew a trail ended, planning on hiking farther in. I glanced in the rear view mirror and saw what looked like a section of the trail begin to move. I couldn't comprehend what I was looking at, so I stopped the car. Whatever it was was crawling across the trail, getting longer and longer. It was brown and yellow, with black two-inch bands around it. And although it never stretched out straight, it covered the road from side to side, a distance of at least ten feet.

Recognition finally hit me. I had seen things this big at the reptile house in several zoos. It was roughly the size of a full grown python.

The eastern timber rattler is the largest rattlesnake in the world. This specimen, left to its own devices in the backwater swamps, had just never stopped growing. I was too stunned to think of grabbing my camera when I got out of the car. I walked toward it, unable to take my eyes from this phenomenon.

Just before its head reached the brush at the far side of the road, it noticed me and began to coil. Its rattles began to quiver, sounding like an oversized set of maracas. By the time I was five feet from it, the snake was poised and set to strike. I felt perfectly safe. I had heard somewhere that snakes can only extend themselves one-third of their total length to strike a target and must face it directly to hit. I have since learned that I was wrong. Their extension is considerably greater, they can strike at any angle in any direction, and do not need to coil before striking. Perhaps my brash ignorance startled the creature. It could not have been used to a challenge of any kind, considering its size.

I stood quite still for several minutes, lost in admiration, before it began to uncurl and moved off into the brush. Back at Flamingo, my story was met with smiles and nods. The park rangers had learned that fishermen are not the only people who exaggerate from time to time. I had no proof, of course, and the rangers found it hard to believe that an experienced woodsman might be too stunned to pick up a camera.

Tales of odd creatures living in the wilderness have persisted throughout recorded history and, whether fact or fantasy, they add an enjoyable mystery to these areas. The state of Washington has passed a law making it illegal to hunt a Sasquatch, supposedly a huge, hairy half-man that inhabits the forests of the Great Northwest. Legends of the Everglades tell of a similar creature, called the skunk ape. Hundreds of sightings have been reported, but there is no physical evidence.

My own credibility—at least with the rangers—went up a notch when I came up with solid evidence of an animal that had presumably deserted the area decades before.

I was on an overnight hike, miles into the swamp, following an abandoned trail. The constant mutterings of unseen life had lulled me into that curious state of both awareness and acceptance. Suddenly, I heard a tremendous noise, a scuffle, and saw a pale brown streak bound across the road ahead of me. Hurrying to the spot where it had disappeared, I recognized, clearly marked in the mud beside the trail, a gigantic cat print. It had to be a puma, the large North American cat that had, by all reckoning, been hunted and driven to near extinction.

I brought a ranger back with me this time, to check the print. He agreed. Since then there have been several sightings of a big, catlike creature disappearing into the shadows—two or three every year. There is probably a small family of pumas living unmolested in the Everglades. It is hoped that they will hang on and perhaps establish the species in the Glades once again. It is a beautiful animal, not at all aggressive to man. I was thrilled to have identified one.

The true glory of the Glades came to me that evening, as I drove back toward Flamingo. A gradual rise took me to treetop level, and for a moment I stood between night and day. To the right, everything in view was a fiery crimson as the sun was settling onto the horizon. And to my left, a full moon had risen, turning half the world to silver.

I stopped, got out, and climbed to the top of the car. The desolate beauty, changing slowly as the sun retreated, drew a familiar fantasy to mind: I was the first man ever to touch this spot, and the armies that would struggle through the wilderness were as yet unborn.

The renewed public interest in our wilderness areas is a two-edged sword. When a few people tramp over a trail every day, little is changed. But when the number swells to eight or ten thousand, the trail dies and eventually the wilderness ceases to exist. People tend to spread and, inadvertently, bring destruction with them. Lights are installed, along with drinking fountains, curio shops, and toilet facilities. And with so many people using the water supply, which may be fragile in these areas, it is inevitable that detergents are returned to the system.

The more popular parks, Yellowstone, for example, are beginning to resemble Disneyland. It is wonderful that so many people want to visit the wilderness, but they are changing it. There seems no reasonable solution to this problem, and many questions involving conservation are still being debated.

Sarina Wasserman has been a close friend of mine for several years. She's a speech pathologist and has a wide range of interests. I wanted to show her the Everglades, so we made plans to fly to Florida for the July Fourth weekend in 1978. Getting away from the office for a few days always involves an incredible number of details, but on the last day of June I was all set to leave. Nothing could go wrong. Then I learned that sloshing through a swamp is an absolute breeze, compared to simply getting out of Manhattan on the day before a holiday.

Sarina arrived at the office in plenty of time to make our flight, but just as I was picking up my bags, an emergency case came in. Dr. Woods was at lunch, so I handled it.

By the time I had cleaned up and was once again ready to leave, we had forty minutes to catch the plane. And because of the holiday, every other flight to Florida was booked solid. We grabbed a cab and headed for the Midtown Tunnel. Every vehicle owner in New York must have had the same idea. Twenty minutes later, we were two blocks from the office. Even at top speed, there was no way we could make it.

"Got an idea," I said, and paid the cabbie. We leaped out in the middle of the block, bags in hand, and raced across the street to the Thirty-third Street heliport.

"I like helicopters," she said, "even less than I like airplanes."

"Close your eyes. Pretend it's a crosstown bus."

We approached the desk. "When does the next copter leave for LaGuardia?" I asked.

The attendant looked up. "They don't leave from here anymore," he said, "you'll have to go down to the Pan Am Building. We just run charters. Trips around the city, stuff like that."

Several helicopters were sitting on the landing strip. One had just come in, and the rotors were still whirling. I pointed to it. "I'd like to charter that," I said, "for about ten minutes."

"Eighty-five bucks."

"That's robbery."

"That's business."

I paid him and we raced out to the helicopter. For that kind of money, you'd think he might have at least carried our bags. While we tossed our luggage into the back, he gave the pilot instructions, and we took off.

The pilot radioed ahead while we were in the air, and arranged for a limousine to meet us at the General Aviation Terminal, which is about half a mile from the Main Terminal. When we landed, the limo was there. We hustled from one vehicle to the other in true V.I.P. fashion while people in the area gawked. I did my best to fulfill the image of a busy diplomat, but Sarina ruined the whole thing. She got the giggles.

We spent the first night with my sister, Alice, in Fort Lauderdale, then drove the last one hundred miles to Flamingo. The incredible mass of living material in the Glades was spectacular, and just as I remembered it— hot, humid, and unearthly beautiful.

The park rangers had started running Swamp Tromps, taking small groups of people into the Glades for a more personal look at the ecology. We joined one that was headed for an area that I was familiar with. I wanted to find a particular twelve-foot alligator, nick-named Ali by the rangers, that I had handfed several times in the past.

Evidently, he had been around long enough to realize that biting the hand that feeds you brings an end to free lunches. Alligators are not as vicious as crocodiles, but hunger will increase their aggressiveness. Their jaws close with tremendous power, and their method of attack is simple, direct, and effective. They grab a victim— occasionally a human—drag him underwater until he drowns, then park the body until it ripens. The alligator grows to a length of about eighteen feet, roughly a foot a year for the first few years. Their average life span is somewhere between thirty and fifty years.

I first encountered Ali eight or nine years ago, near a small pond not far from Flamingo. I tossed him some food, and he seemed mildly responsive. Over the years, on successive visits, I recognized him and began to trust him a little more. Each time I moved closer and stayed longer. For fifty yards, an alligator can move overland at roughly thirty miles an hour—a good clip, even for an Olympic-class runner. It's not against the law to hand-feed them, but it's not a very good idea.

Ali didn't show up on this trip. I was throwing some bread and crackers to another 'gator when a ranger came up and said, "That baby attacked a visitor a week ago. We caught him, moved him to a deeper part of the Glades, and two days later he was back." Two other alligator attacks were reported while we were there, and I began to revise my thinking about befriending the creatures.

We got up very early the next morning and went out alone looking for sinkholes. They are the Glades version of African waterholes and are dug by 'gators in search of fresh water during the dry season. With repeated use over a decade or so, some of them grow to the size of small lakes. Back when the upstate canal system was going in and the water level sank, the 'gators dug them as deep as ten feet, and all they were getting was salt water.

We found a large one, just at dawn. Very quietly we climbed a hillock and sat with binoculars watching one of the true wonders of nature. Hundreds of alligators, thousands of birds, and millions of fish, all concentrated in this small area. We spotted a number of giant turtles among the wild lilacs that ringed the scene; an occasional sea otter cavorted undisturbed among the alligators.

The screams of death and life, feeding and survival, silenced both of us. Wading through hip-deep water for miles to observe this spectacular ritual of nature would not appeal to everyone. It is, of course, possible to appreciate the Glades with no more risk than watching television. But even fifty yards from the beaten trails it becomes a different world. And it's worth the effort.

10

On the Other End
of the Leash

Most of the pet owners and animal people that I have met and worked with seem to have a natural compassion for the creatures that share our earth. But odd ducks can be found on either end of the leash and range from the pleasantly eccentric to those of questionable sanity.

My first brush with this darker side of human nature occurred shortly after I got out of college and was working with Dr. Kessler in Brooklyn. It was after midnight and I was in the office alone. I had been up most of the previous night on an emergency and was about ready to pack it in when I heard someone beating on the outer door. I went to answer it. Two men came in, carrying what was left of a Great Dane.

"In here," I said, leading them toward surgery.

The dog was in shock, literally spurting blood from a dozen wounds. I attached hemostats and quickly began tying them off to keep the dog from bleeding to death on the table.

The men, both soaked with blood from the dog, told me what had happened as I worked. They were on the night shift at a Brooklyn factory and had seen the dog hit head-on by a car. The owner, a middle-aged man they had often seen walking his dog late at night in the area, went to pieces. They offered to help. Placing the animal in the back of the company station wagon, they raced to the nearest hospital.

At the emergency ward they learned that human hospitals do not treat wounded animals. They were told to call a vet, but in the excitement they simply took off to find one, the owner in one direction, the station wagon in the other. They had no idea where the owner was, or when he would show up.

By the time I could start pumping whole blood into the dog, the office looked like a slaughterhouse. The floors were slippery with blood, and we were all covered with it. After three hours of surgery, there was no logical reason why the dog was still alive. The factory workers knew they would catch hell from their boss for taking off with the company car, but once involved, they found it impossible just to turn and walk away. I was nearly finished with the dog, and beyond the point of exhaustion myself, when the owner found us.

In our haste we had left the front door ajar. He walked in and followed the trail of blood directly to surgery. He was disheveled and looking a bit wild-eyed but otherwise seemed to be an average citizen whose pet had fallen prey to one of the hazards of civilization.

"I'll do anything to save my dog," he said, "anything you want."

"I'm not sure he'll make it. He's pretty badly busted up."

With barely a nod to the men who had brought his dog in, he turned and began pacing nervously throughout the office.

"I can understand how he feels," said one of the men. "I lost a collie the same way, last year."

"There isn't much more I can do for him right now," I said. "I'll keep him under observation and turn him over to Dr. Kessler when he gets in."

The owner appeared at the door, frowning. "How long is this going to take?" he asked, "I have an appointment at nine, and I want to take the dog home first."

I paused a moment, then said, "Well, you won't be able to move the dog. He's in bad shape. He'd die the minute you got him out of here."

He looked at the three of us suspiciously. "I want the dog. And I don't want no shit from you!"

I couldn't believe his sudden change in attitude. The larger of the two workers raised his hand. "Take it easy, fellow," he said.

Ignoring him, the owner stared straight at me and launched into a rambling speech, the main point of which seemed to be that veterinarians spend most of their waking hours devising ways to rip off the public.

I was getting pretty close to the skin by then. After five hours of surgery, my self-control was at something of a low ebb. "If you want to kill your dog, go ahead and take it," I said. I wrote him out a bill. It was absurdly low, considering the work involved.

He grabbed it out of my hand and studied it. "I'll only pay fifteen dollars," he said.

That would have covered about half the cost of the blood I had administered to the dog. "You want to owe the rest, right?"

"I don't want to owe anything. I'll pay you fifteen bucks, and I want a signed paper that says I don't owe anything."

"We didn't give up a night's work so you could kill the dog," said the worker. "Pay the vet, leave the dog, and beat it!"

"It's my dog! I'll do whatever I want with it!"

They both started yelling.

The younger worker and I exchanged a glance. "I think maybe I'll leave," he said.

"Me, too."

The Great Dane's owner suddenly swung at his opponent and was unceremoniously decked. He scrambled to his feet. We leaped between them, and everyone froze.

The sun was just coming up over Long Island. Birds along the tree-lined street began to stir. Another perfect day was off to a running start.

Pulling free of my grasp, the owner rubbed his unmarked chin, marched to the phone, and called the police. "A veterinarian is trying to kill me," he said calmly. "They kidnapped my dog, beat me up in the office, and won't let me out. Would you please send somebody down?" He gave them the address, and hung up.

I began to wonder what on earth I was doing there, standing in a bloodbath, listening to a very rational-sounding madman accuse me of every major crime this side of murder. For a moment, I considered adding murder to the list.

"Mind if I use the phone?" I asked.

He moved away from the desk, folding his arms in a you're-gonna-get-yours attitude. The men from the factory both sat down. What had been a long night was obviously going to be extended.

I dialed Dr. Kessler. "Hi, Sid. It's Mike."

"Mike. Right. I thought I set my alarm. It's light outside. Did I oversleep?"

"It's okay, Sid. It's only six."

"Why'd you call me?"

"If I said I had an emergency operation and needed help, would you come right over?"

"Of course. What kind of operation?"

"The operation's over. But there's blood all over the floor. And there's a guy here yelling that he's been beaten up and kidnapped. And there's a Great Dane dying in surgery. And the cops are gonna be here in a minute. How about dropping in?"

Within five minutes he was in the door, still buttoning his coat over his pajamas. Just as he got the first dozen questions out of his mouth, we heard sirens approaching.

The dog owner took off his coat, ripped his shirt open, then fell down on the floor and started smearing blood all over himself—in his hair, on his face and clothes, everywhere he could reach.

"What's wrong with him?" asked Dr. Kessler.

"He's okay," I said, "just kind of nuts."

Two police officers walked in. The man on the floor

began writing around, screaming, "Oh! My heart! They kicked me! They beat me!"

The senior policeman took one look at him and said, "Phony." His partner nodded agreement, and they turned their attention to the rest of us to find out what had happened.

"How did you know?" I said. "I mean, you're right —but how could you tell?"

"After twenty years on the force, you can smell 'em." Ignoring the owner, who had redoubled his histrionics, the officers listened to our unlikely story. Several other patrol cars pulled up out front, and the peaceful Brooklyn neighborhood began to look like the site of Bonnie and Clyde's last stand.

Satisfied that his first analysis was correct, the policeman went over to talk to the pet owner. "Heart attack, huh? Well, we'll get you to a hospital. Somebody call an ambulance."

"Wait. I feel a little better."

"A little better?"

"Yes. A lot better, in fact." He started wiping the blood off himself.

"Don't touch the blood," said the policeman, "we'll have it analyzed. Want to find out who beat you up."

"Gee, I might have tripped, you know. And it splashed on me, from the dog."

"What seems to be the trouble, then?"

"I just want to take my dog." He got to his feet.

The policeman turned to me. "And your statement, Doctor, is that the dog will die if it's moved?"

"Yes. Definitely. The dog may die, even if it stays here. I don't know why it's still alive, as it is. He needs at least another couple hours of blood dripping into him, if nothing else."

"You still want the dog?"

The owner nodded.

"It's his dog. He can do whatever he wants," I said.

"All right," said the officer, "pay your bill, and let's all go home."

"Oh, no. I won't pay more than fifteen dollars."

"Let's give him the dog," said Sid.

"Fine," I said, "no charge. It was a wonderful evening."

The owner looked satisfied. He wiped a little more blood off his face and said, "Would you help me carry him out to the car?"

The factory workers looked at each other in disbelief and walked out.

We carried the dog out to the car, an old coupe. The back seat, from floor to window, was filled with slops. Wet, garbagey stuff, normally fed to pigs. And sitting in the slops, with his head barely visible, was another Great Dane.

When the stench hit us, we almost dropped the animal.

"Where . . . should we put it?" asked the officer.

"In the back. With the other dog."

"What's that in your car?" I asked.

"That's what I feed my dogs," he said, "I get it cheap."

"And you want us to put this animal in it?"

"Just put him in! And believe me, the city officials are going to hear about how I've been treated tonight!"

The police opened the door and put the dog in. The

last I saw of him, he was sinking down into the slops. They slowly began to turn red with the blood oozing out of him.

The man drove off.

For a moment, we all just stood there.

"Sid," I said, "I'm gonna wake up soon. This just didn't happen."

"Why don't you get washed up and put on a clean shirt," he said, "and we'll go have some breakfast."

People have a remarkable capacity for ignoring facts and believing exactly what they want to believe, even if there is overwhelming evidence to the contrary. One of the most unhappy aspects of my profession is clarifying, to a client, the actual physical state of their pet. Sometimes an owner will bring in an animal they have had for many years. It might be suffering from arthritis, heart murmur, partial blindness—all the symptoms of advancing age. And even if the situation is hopeless, they are often unwilling to face the possibility that euthanasia might be the kindest way to end the animal's suffering.

They don't want to say it; they want the vet to suggest it, to relieve them of whatever guilt they may feel. I usually sit down and talk to them and, during the conversation, mention it as a viable alternative. But I always leave the final decision up to them. For my first five years of practice I absolutely forbade an owner being present when I administered the injection. The emotional reaction of putting an old friend to sleep, I felt, would be lessened by not watching. But for those clients who feel it will be easier for their pet if they are there, I now explain the procedure carefully and allow them in.

Most owners outlive their pets, of course, and the emotional trauma involved with losing one can be extreme—as in the case of Mrs. M.

Mrs. M. called for an appointment for her dog, a mixed-breed mutt we had had as a regular patient for several years. She got out of a cab and dragged her dog, on a leash, across the sidewalk and into the office. She coaxed him along, saying "Come on, boy. Come on. The doctor's going to give you a shot and make you all well."

She was a lovely, elderly woman who lived alone with her dog and was incapable of harming a fly. But by the time she reached the desk, the clients in our waiting room were huddled up against the wall.

"What seems to be wrong?" asked our secretary.

"My dog has been very listless," said Mrs. M.

The dog was stiffer than a lawn ornament.

"How long . . . has he been like this?"

"Well, about four days. I'd like Dr. Milts to give him a shot, and make him well."

I answered the intercom, and came to the front office. She told me the same story. Her eyes were glowing with faith and hope.

"Perhaps you should leave him with us for a few days," I said.

"I couldn't do that," she said gently. "He just doesn't sleep well away from home."

Everyone in the room was silent, waiting for me to explain that the dog was dead.

"I'll give him some medicine," I said.

I picked the dog up, carried him into a recovery room, waited a minute or two, then brought him back out.

She took the dog in her arms, then turned to the secretary to pay her bill.

"What should I put down?"

"Uh, no charge."

Mrs. M. looked at me strangely.

"We have a lot of extra medicine laying around," I said.

She thanked me, attached the leash to the collar, and dragged her dog out the door.

Two days later, she called back. She had bad news for us. One of her neighbors had come over for a visit and had convinced her that, despite our wonderful efforts, her dog had passed away.

"I'm really sorry to hear that," I said. I was.

"But do you think he would have had a chance, if I'd left him in the hospital?"

I assured her that nothing further could have been done, and the dog was undoubtedly happier, during its last hours, getting her care and affection.

Pets sometimes become pawns in the complicated game of chess that people play with their own relationships. I have yet to meet a veterinarian who does not have his share of such stories—horror stories, really—to tell. We had two strangely similar ones at the office within a period of six months.

A large, burly fellow walked into the office one afternoon carrying a cardboard box. With obvious distaste, he shoved it at us. It contained a skunk with a broken leg. It belonged to his girlfriend, he said. A broom had fallen over and injured it.

We set the bone and fashioned a splint. All the while

he sat in the waiting room mumbling to himself, wondering "how anyone could own such an animal."

He brought it back a week later. It had wounds on the chest, as if it had been kicked repeatedly.

"It fell down a flight of stairs," he said.

I treated it again. Considering the basic personality of your average descented skunk, it was an exceptionally quiet and friendly little animal; young and agile enough, certainly, to rule out the possibility of falling down stairs.

The third time he brought it in was more serious. It had third degree burns all over its body, and I noticed that both his hands were bandaged. This time, his excuse was that he had tried to give it a bath.

It seemed to have little chance to live. We had to keep it for a month and pulled it through. Then the girlfriend, the owner, came in to pick it up.

Legally, there is a thousand dollar fine involved for keeping pets in New York that are indigenous to the forest. It is rarely invoked, but it is on the books. I told her, quite honestly, that I thought her boyfriend was abusing the animal, and that she could save both vet bills and a fine by finding an out-of-city home for it.

The idea that her friend might be jealous of a skunk was a bit farfetched, of course. But, without too much trouble, I was able to convince her that the animal would be happier elsewhere. I wound up taking it to the Brook's sanctuary for animals, where it recovered, and was able to roam freely near a barn where it could find food and shelter.

It couldn't have been more than a week later that another girl brought in her cat with a broken leg. As her story unfolded it became almost an instant replay of the skunk incident.

Over a period of just a few weeks, she brought it back with cuts, with bruises, with a swollen eye, and eventually with burns. The final time, she came in crying and quite shaken.

"I can't go home anymore," she said, after I had treated the cat. Her boyfriend had a key to her apartment, and she had walked in and found him trying to scald the cat to death.

"Maybe he's jealous," I said, "things like that happen to children often enough. Why not pets? Is the guy violent by nature, or what?"

"He's a wonderful guy. He's really warm and gentle. He said if I took the cat to the vet again, he's going to throw me out the window."

"If I were you, I don't think I'd take the cat home. We'll keep it here and put it up for adoption, if you want."

Seeing that she was going to marry this man, she agreed that getting rid of the cat would be the best solution. As she was leaving, I added, "Lady, I hope he never gets jealous of you."

There is very little that can legally be done about such incidents of animal cruelty. But the time it happened in our office, the clients took matters into their own hands.

The waiting room was crowded the day this young couple brought in their five-week-old Yorkshire terrier for shots. The man didn't like the office, didn't like waiting, but most of all, he didn't like the animal that was sitting on his lap making frightened puppy sounds.

He started complaining loudly and was soon yelling at the dog, which of course only made it worse. Clients began edging away from him while his wife attempted, unsuccessfully, to calm him down.

I came up front to check on the confusion and got there just in time to see him double up his fist and bring it down on the dog's head, killing it instantly.

The woman started screaming.

The man stood up, and the lifeless puppy slipped off his lap and hit the floor. Our clients, men and women alike, surged toward the startled man and began beating him with fist, purse, umbrella, and everything else they could lay their hands on.

He fled, followed shortly by his angry wife. I sincerely hope she caught him.

Whenever Clem and Jethro were in town, their handlers brought them in for a routine examination. They were magnificent gray wolves weighing about a hundred pounds apiece, and as nearly domesticated as wolves ever get. They were taken around the country in a special exhibit, primarily to teach people that although the wolf is not a house pet, neither is it a vicious, horrid creature to be automatically exterminated.

When they were first brought in for observation, we kept them in a cage that had stainless steel bars. Nothing short of a grizzly should be able to break through that. But the next morning, when Marty came in to work, he found them curled up and sleeping peacefully in the hallway.

They just didn't like being locked up. They had taken

the bars in their teeth, bent them into pretzels, and ripped them loose. After that, they were allowed to roam the office at night.

About a year later, I got a call from Cleveland Amory, who has publicly fought animal cruelty for many years. We had become close friends through our mutual interest in this and other projects. With his usual enthusiasm, he had gotten deeply involved in the traveling wolf exhibition. He sounded quite grim on the phone. The wolves were writhing in agony and vomiting. I told him to bring the wolves in immediately. They died in the office. Someone had thrown poisoned meat into their cage.

After some investigation, the police found the person responsible: an elderly woman who was eventually released into the custody of her relatives. But she told the court, "I'm really sorry. I didn't know they were wolves. If I had known that, I never would have done it. I thought they were dogs."

Long John Nebel was a radio personality for many years in New York. He and his wife, Candy Jones, hosted a late-night talk show on a local station, WMCA. Interviewing off-beat people became their hallmark, and a whole procession of UFO-logists, bag ladies, and other strange professionals appeared on the show. They were also animal people, and I joined them for a chat on a number of occasions. Long John died last year, unfortunately, but Candy took over the show and is continuing it for their large and enthusiastic following.

She was in the office one afternoon several years ago and was standing by the tiered cages of cats on display for adoption. One of the cats, a tabby that had been brought in from the streets several weeks before reached out and hooked her sweater with its claws. The two of them stared at each other for a moment.

"Hi, Mom!" said Candy.

The cat began to purr.

Candy turned to the secretary and said, "That's my mother. The one in the second cage, there. Could you lend me a carrier? I'd like to take her home."

There was a long silence in the waiting room, then Candy continued matter-of-factly, "I'm so happy I found her. I had a dream that I would see my mother today. She died a good many years ago, and that's obviously her, come back. You can just tell it, looking in those eyes."

"Bill," I said, "would you please take Candy's mother out of the cage?"

Without the flicker of an eyelid, Bill brought out a pet carrier.

On the program a few weeks later, the subject of cats came up. Candy said, "You know, a lot of people don't believe in reincarnation. It's a controversial subject. But I do, and I was in Dr. Milts's office, and I saw my mother in one of his cages. So naturally, I adopted her. It's really nice. We get along terrifically."

After she had left that first day, one of our other clients sidled up to me and said, "Do you have those cats trained to reach out and grab customers?"

"No," I said, "but—you know how mothers are."

I met the Lee sisters when I was practicing in Brooklyn. Two very genteel, fragile ladies who live in a lovely house full of antiques, paintings, parrots, cats, and Stormy.

Stormy is healthy, active, good-natured, and probably the biggest Great Dane in the world. Much too big for them to handle, and a definite problem whenever they want to bring him in for treatment or shots. Neither of them drives, and Stormy won't fit into the back of a taxi.

For a while, they solved the problem by simply calling an ambulance, a regular human ambulance service. But after the first few trips, the ambulance service cut them off, claiming they were much too busy picking up people. Stormy found travel very exciting, and there were no attendants brave enough to try strapping him down.

Nowadays, they call Marty, at home. Sometimes with symptoms, and sometimes just to have someone to talk to. He listens patiently, and if it seems warranted, he'll pick up the dog in his car the next morning.

"You're going to get a phone call," he will say, struggling through the door with the delighted behemoth straining to greet us from the leash, and sure enough, the phone will ring. Invariably, it is one of the sisters, calling to redescribe Stormy's condition.

Once Marty had to double-park to pick up the dog, and when he came out of the house, a policeman was there writing out a ticket. The Lees spotted him, flew from the house, and surrounded him. "He's a neighbor," they exclaimed, "just picking up our dog to take him in for treatment! You can't give him a ticket for that!"

The officer could and did.

"That's disgusting!" one of them shouted, "This man is an angel of mercy!"

"We'll take it to court!" yelled the other.

They made good their threat, and after an impassioned plea—invoking all that was good, fair, beautiful, and just—the magistrate reduced the fine. If he was not a dog lover before the case came up, he certainly was afterwards.

11
Short Change

Barnaby sprawled like a great shaggy mountain in the middle of the waiting room. Patients and pets scampered over and around him, clients stepped carefully near the walls, and the din of frightened and excited animals made conversation nearly impossible. He slept throughout the chaos.

It was one of those hot days in the late summer when people tend to get irritable. Appointments had backed up, new clients had strolled in unannounced, and we had more than our share of mystery clients—animals brought in by owners who state, "My dog is sick; please check him out," and then walk out without giving us a clue as to what might possibly be wrong.

Tempers shortened as the temperature rose. The

office menagerie, a collection of freewheeling misfit cats, picked up the mood. Clarence raced from room to room, turning on water faucets with his paw. Subway, who would be certifiably insane if born human rather than feline, spent his morning happily attacking every leg that scurried by him down the corridor. By ten o'clock Bill had to shut both of them in the cellar. Their howls of outrage only added to the confusion.

Then just before noon we had an emergency that seemed to turn the day around for everyone on the staff as well as the clients who were present. A little dark-haired girl, eight or nine years old, walked in carrying a matchbox.

She stood by the door a minute, looking scared and nervous, then made her way to the desk. Carefully, she sat the matchbox down in front of Caroline and slid it open. Inside, on a bed of cotton, perched a healthy-looking cricket. It seemed quite content. There was no discernable expression of pain in any of its twelve eyes.

"What's wrong?" asked Caroline.

"It has a broken arm," said the little girl.

Caroline looked closer. It began to move. And sure enough, one of the legs on its thorax jutted out at a crazy angle.

"The second one on the left, there?"

The little girl nodded solemnly.

Caroline picked up the intercom. "Dr. Milts, we have an emergency up front," she said.

"Be right out." I was just washing up, after restoring a badly constipated turtle to some measure of regularity. Bill came in to remove the turtle. He is a quiet person, rather shy, and in control of his emotions. But he had a big grin on his face.

"What's up?"

"Short change," he said, meaning we had a very small animal to treat.

In the waiting room, I found the clients crowded around the desk, discussing the case. Caroline motioned toward the matchbox and I peered in. "Bill," I said, "could you get me a tongue depressor?"

The clients smirked, conjuring up, I suppose, the image of a veterinarian telling a cricket to "open your mouth and say ahhh."

When Bill returned, I shaved a minuscule sliver of wood from the tongue depressor, fashioned a splint, and secured it to the errant leg with a tiny strip of gauze.

When I finished, Caroline wrote up a bill and gave a copy to the client. There is no going rate for cricket repair. We chalked it up to experience. And the manufacture of butterflies.

In our rush to turn the world into a parking lot, we have done our best to ignore the lesser in stature of our fellow creatures. They are often better adapted for survival than we are and will doubtless prevail—through sheer numbers, if for no other reason—long after we have passed.

A closer encounter with some of the smaller species rarely fails to interest the layman. Whenever I bring my vivarium, containing a tarantula and a scorpion, into the office, clients who get panicky at a kitten's sneeze sit fascinated, watching them feed.

A tarantula's sight is a lot worse than its bite, which

is no more harmful to man than a pinprick. But because it is large, hairy, and fierce looking, the legend of its deadliness will probably persist. Mine is quite a gentle creature, about five inches long (if you include the legs) and actually looks too big for the vivarium. But her natural habitat wouldn't cover much more territory. In the wilds a tarantula is often born, lives, and dies within a single square foot of land. And they sometimes live more than twenty years. Some of the larger tropical species are more venomous; I've seen them in groups of more than a hundred on back roads in Yucatan, but the bite of even the largest is more an annoyance than a danger.

Tara, my pet tarantula, is slow moving and sluggish by nature—until a few crickets or a small mouse is put into the vivarium. Then she leaps, stings, and is feeding in seconds.

The scorpion is a different matter altogether. It is not aggressive toward man unless threatened, and some species are harmless. But others inject a nerve poison that is fatal. Their method of feeding is as graceful as a dance. The arm extends, plucking up a passing cricket, the tail arches up and over the body to administer the deadly sting. Another claw grabs another cricket, and the tail loops over again. If it hasn't eaten for several weeks, which is not unusual, it can handle up to four crickets at a time. The victims move through an assembly line of pincher and sting, then are eventually parked on little stalks that surround the scorpion's mouth.

I don't normally keep poisonous pets, but the one who shares the vivarium with my tarantula has sentimental value. Even though the sentiments involved are somewhat suspect.

About a year after Florence and I separated, I began dating an attractive blonde named Joan. We had known each other for a number of years, and when we both rejoined the ranks of the uncommitted, we began to see each other. Over a period of months Joan became more serious about our relationship, while I just wasn't ready for another long-term alliance. Things cooled off, and we drifted apart.

Months later, she called and suggested we get together for an evening, as she had a present for me. I picked up tickets to a musical and we went out. At intermission she took a small box from her purse and gave it to me.

"Here's a playmate for your tarantula," she said. "It's one of the harmless species, but you should partition it off."

"What is it?"

"A scorpion. Very gentle. You can pick it up, hand-feed it, and everything."

I thanked her and, when I got home, divided the vivarium and dumped it in. It was beautiful; a pale beige, with darker stripes on the back, and about three inches long. I fed it crickets. But not by hand.

That was the last I heard from Joan for several months. Then one night I was awakened by a phone call. Sleepily, I answered.

"Oh," she said, "I guess you haven't been playing with your scorpion." And she hung up.

The next morning I began to wonder about her strange call, and I phoned a friend at Small World, the pet store where she had bought it. The owner told me what had happened.

A beautiful blonde had floated in one day and asked a few questions about venomous creatures. They had a scorpion on exhibit, but it wasn't for sale because it was one of the deadly species.

"Oh, it's for Dr. Milts," she said, "he'll know how to take care of it. It's a present. For his vivarium."

"We wouldn't have sold it, Mike, if we had known it was going to anyone else," the owner explained to me. "How's it doing, anyway?"

"Fine," I said, "just fine. I just wanted to check the species." I hung up and dialed Joan.

"You tried to kill me," I said.

"It might not have killed you," she said, "maybe just put you in the hospital for a nice long stretch. Why do you sound so upset?"

"It could have killed me. Dead."

"You already said that. I hate people who harp. Talk about something else."

"But if I had fed it—"

She hung up, obviously bored with my conversation.

Nearly a year later, she called from California. She had changed jobs and moved out to the coast. But she would be in New York for a couple of days on business, she said, and offered to come over to the house and cook up an exotic dinner. She would even pick up the ingredients.

I apologized. I had already made plans for that weekend. Whenever it was.

Some presents have not been as hard to take as the scorpion, which I named Joan, obviously for sentimental reasons.

In the late 1960s, for better or worse, I began to get a reputation as a veterinarian who treats exotic animals not many other doctors wanted to deal with. One wouldn't think that any of the forty species of gull, the scavenger bird so common to coastal regions, could be considered exotic. But even though their habits have been studied, few are kept as pets, so knowledge of their treatment is scant.

One day I got a call from a silky-voiced woman who was spending her summer at her estate, far down the New Jersey shoreline. She had been walking on the beach and came across a baby seagull. The mother was nowhere in sight, so she took it home. Having no idea of how to feed it, she had called the local vet. He had never treated a seagull but referred her to another vet. The second passed her to a third, who suggested a fourth. I was number fifteen.

I promised to find out what I could and asked her to call back the following day. It was an interesting problem, but unfortunately, there was little time to experiment. The herring gull was starving to death, and I learned that the feeding procedure of this species is unique.

The mother gull chews up the food, partially digests it, then regurgitates it. But to trigger this response, the chick must see, and peck at, a small red spot on the lower bill of the adult.

When she called back, I advised the woman to put a dot of nail polish on an eyedropper to simulate the mothers beak. The chick responded properly. The phone calls continued for several days as we tried a variety of artificial formulas to provide a proper diet.

She was up at all hours, mulching the different concoctions I suggested in her blender, but time ran out on us, and the baby gull succumbed.

About a week later, the longest limousine I'd ever seen drove up in front of the office. A stunningly beautiful woman stepped out, walked into the waiting room, and introduced herself. "I'm the seagull lady," she said.

We spent a few minutes unhappily discussing the case, then she thanked me for my time and trouble, and left me a bottle of sixty-year-old cognac.

"Excuse me, sir," the waitress in the little coffee shop said, "but your bag just twitched."

The four of us looked at her as though she was out of her mind. We had stopped in for a cup of espresso on our way to the theater, and I had brought along a brown paper lunchbag to deliver at a nearby apartment.

"Twitched?" I said, looking around at my friends.

They shrugged innocently. The waitress took our order and soon returned with coffee and pastry. She served us, carefully avoiding the bag. And just as she was ready to leave, the bag twitched again.

"Mister, that bag moved."

"They must have woke up," said one of my friends.

"It must be feeding time," said another.

"Do you have any mice?" I asked the waitress, "My boa constrictors are hungry."

She smiled dubiously. I opened the top of the sack, and she peeked in. She stared for a full ten seconds. Then, very quietly, she made out our check and laid it on the table. Glancing at our coffee cups, she said "No refills," and disappeared into the kitchen. We didn't see her again.

The boas were only babies, each about eight inches long and harmless. John Fitzgerald breeds them as a sideline and had asked me to deliver them to a customer after I had looked them over that day. Rather than carting around a bulky cage, I had slipped them into the paper bag.

After finishing our coffee, we left the money for the bill—plus a generous tip—on the table and went to drop off the snakes. In the lobby of the apartment building, we got to joking about the way the waitress had reacted. I must have mentioned the person we were delivering them to, because a young girl waiting for the elevator suddenly looked horrified.

"The things in the bag—they're going up *there?*"

"Sure," I said.

"But—I'm supposed to babysit for them tonight!"

We assured her that there was no possible way the snakes could harm her, but she refused to go up in the same elevator with us. "What if we get stuck between floors?" she said.

She took the first elevator up, and we followed on the next. When we arrived, she was just finishing a loud and indignant speech charging the customers with attempted murder. "And that guy," she said, pointing a finger at me, "said he was bringing you Mexican jumping beans!"

I ended up apologizing to everyone, including the building superintendent and the doorman. The pet lovers ended up locking the sack of boas in a closet for the evening. And the babysitter ended up making three times her usual fee.

12
Zoo Follies

Zoo animals are well fed and protected. Their incidence of breeding may be lower than in the wilds, but so is the mortality rate for both infant and adult. Any number of times I've seen visitors to the Central Park Zoo observe Raunchy the lion relaxing majestically in his cage and comment, "Boy, he's got it made!"

In some cases it's true; some species adapt well to life in a zoo and even seem to thrive on it. But for others, especially those gathered from a different natural climate, life is more precarious. They are subjected to infections they are not physically equipped to fight. Respiratory ailments are common, and diseases may be picked up from animals in nearby cages or even from visitors to the zoo. And sometimes the disease is so rare to a species that diagnosis is impossible until a post-mortem is done.

One steamy summer evening, just as I was preparing to go out for a late dinner date, Fitzgerald called from Central Park. The jaguar, he said, seemed to be in pain, although there was nothing overtly wrong with it. Could I come over and take a look?

I called my date and told her I would be delayed, then packed up and headed for the zoo. The prospect of a quiet dinner in an air-conditioned restaurant began to fade once I saw the animal. It crouched near the back of the cage, rheumy-eyed, skittish, and breathing irregularly. From time to time the head would tilt, the jaws would open as though to roar, but no sound came out.

Although we didn't know it at the time, the beautifully marked 250-pound cat had developed lung cancer and would be dead within a very few months.

"What do you think, Mike?" John asked. His dedication to the welfare of the zoo animals has always bordered on that of a doting father.

"I don't really know," I said, "but he's obviously in pain. I'll sedate him and take a blood sample for analysis."

I loaded up the tranquilizer gun with a syringe of ketimine, fired, and waited for the jag to go under. It clawed the dart loose from its rump, but I thought it had taken enough to do the job.

It circled the cage twice, then settled back into its corner. Minutes passed before it began to look glazed.

I unlocked the cage and climbed up to attract its attention and see how much activity it would show. The door was not quite as tall as my head, so I had to duck slightly. The large yellow eyes followed my progress, but the animal didn't move. And just as I stepped into the cage, all the lights in the Central Park Zoo went out. There was a local power failure.

Instinctively, I turned to leave in the vanishing glow of the lightbulb. But in my haste, I simply forgot to duck. My head hit the top of the metal door frame. Stunned, I reeled backward and fell to my hands and knees.

Vaguely I heard John shouting for me to get out of the cage. I didn't seem to be able to stand or even crawl. The last thing I heard before pitching forward on my face was the sound of claws scurrying across the cement floor.

A telephone was ringing in the distance, unanswered. And nearby someone was shouting for a flashlight.

Get up, I thought, swimming back toward consciousness, *and help them look for one.* But somewhere along the line, I had forgotten how to move. And there was a tremendous weight on the back of my neck.

Other panicky voices joined the first.

"Is the cage open?"

"I think the jag got him!"

"Where the hell is a flashlight!"

Gradually I put together the pieces of my existence. My face was covered with a wet, sticky substance. The weight on my neck and shoulders was furry. I had the grandfather of all headaches.

Someone finally located a flashlight and beamed it into the cage. The unconscious jaguar was sprawled on top of me, and I was covered with blood.

"Oh, Christ! It hit him!"

"The door hit me," I said. "Would someone get this damn cat off my back? And answer the phone!"

Two keepers crawled in to rescue me while a third went to get the phone. As I was lifted to my feet, the lights slowly came back on and the room began to spin. I nearly passed out again before they got me out of the cage.

I sat down for a few minutes until the shaking stopped, then washed up and set about getting blood samples from the cat. As I worked, my date came rushing in.

"I called when the blackout hit," she said. "Some guy said you were busy being attacked by a jaguar and hung up."

We explained what had actually happened and agreed that if the jaguar had remained conscious for another thirty seconds, I would have, quite literally, lost my head.

We dressed my wound, which was superficial even though it bled quite a lot. I walked around for a week with a large knot on my head. But the jaguar's condition worsened; it quit eating and had to be fed intravenously. X-rays showed the cancer far too advanced for any kind of treatment to be of help. We finally had to euthanize it to end the suffering.

Not all animals come to the zoo in tip-top shape. Each is given a thorough physical upon arrival, though a veterinary certificate, attached to every bill of lading should note anything out of the ordinary. Theoretically, each animal has been carefully examined by a registered vet before it is shipped.

On June 4, 1978, the Central Park Zoo received two young capybaras from an animal dealer in Venezuela. Rufus, our previous specimen, had passed away at the ripe old age of ten. He had been, as far as we could ascertain, the largest capybara in captivity. A large adult may reach a weight of 110 pounds; Rufus weighed nearly twice that.

The capybara is the world's largest living rodent, brown in color, sparsely haired, and looking something like a cross between a hippo and a guinea pig.

It was Sunday, normally my day off, but I wanted to be on hand when they arrived. The keepers uncrated them in an outdoor pen while I looked over the veterinary certificate. The only notation was "minor wound" on one of the animals.

Both of them dashed from the crate as soon as it was opened. They are very skittish creatures—a definite attribute for a mild vegetarian species native to the predator-filled jungles of South America. I decided to examine the one with the minor wound first. It took five of us nearly an hour to subdue the frightened animal. It kept squealing, dodging between our legs, out of grasp, and avoiding the corners of the pen. We attracted a small audience who, naturally, cheered for the underdog.

Superior manpower won out in the end, and I finally got a close look at the wound located just below the rib cage. I didn't like it. It looked deep.

I estimated the animal's weight at about thirty pounds and gave it an appropriate anesthetic. I set up my surgery pack with lots of hot water, disinfectant soap, and electric clippers to shave off the hair around the wound. We were working near the fence, in full view of our audience. Several of them crowded up close to watch the operation.

I proceeded to open up the wound. The onlookers dispersed when I took out the first of the maggots.

Certain species of flies lay their eggs in open wounds. The eggs hatch into larvae, and the larvae feed on live tissue, eating their way through the host animal and literally destroying it if left unchecked. I had to make an eight-inch incision, following the tracks of the maggots through the body, to remove all of them. There were more than fifty.

I sutured the wound, put the capybara on antibiotics, but had little hope for its recovery. The stress of shipping, the nervousness of these animals in general, plus the anesthetic and surgery would, I felt, be too much to overcome. But it regained consciousness, snorted, and in a matter of seconds was on its wobbly legs and heading away from us.

The other capybara, or water hog as they are sometimes called, was in better shape, and they have both adapted to life in captivity quite well. But no other animals have been purchased from that particular South American dealer.

Polar bears rarely catch a cold. They are perfectly adapted for life in a climate that—given only his natural resistance—would quickly kill a human. But they are not immune to respiratory ailments, particularly in the summer. And when the temperature soared in New York City in November, 1977, the polar bear, in effect, caught a warm.

For three weeks, he refused to eat. Polars do not

hibernate, but they do store up a good deal of residual fat to carry them through leaner times. He grew steadily weaker and thinner, existing on his own stored resources, and we began to think that we might lose him.

Administering medication was a problem. Normally, medicine would be mixed in with its food. But it wasn't eating, and I was not about to enter the cage of a creature that, hungry or not, would tear me to shreds. So three times a day I came to the zoo with my dart gun and several syringes of antibiotics and vitamins.

The New York City zoos are, in every sense of the word, public. There is no room in the city budget for expansion or treatment facilities, so it is a catch-as-catch-can procedure. And considering the dimensions of the polar bear den in central Park, the emphasis is on "catch."

It's a spectacular arrangement of cliffs, carved into the side of a small mountain, towering sixty feet from base to crest. The bears climb it easily, and at the bottom there is a large pool. They use it to cool off in, when the weather isn't frigid enough to suit them. But this bear hadn't gone near it for weeks, and it was in the process of being drained for cleaning while I was treating him.

As I showed up with the gun, day after day, he began to get wary. All I had to do was walk into sight, and he would head for the farthest corner, or scramble up to the top of what we began to call Bear Mountain. Getting a clear shot at him became more and more difficult. We eventually attracted a regular crowd of onlookers, who began to bet among themselves on whether or not I would actually hit the bear on the first, second, or third shots. It got to be something of a game to them, but it was a losing one to us, as we watched the bear gradually deteriorate in health.

We changed tactics. I would approach the den openly brandishing a tranquilizer gun while another keeper crept up at another angle and hit him at point-blank range with another gun. The bear changed tactics too.

If anyone came near the den carrying anything at all, he would climb to the top, where he had a better view of these little creatures that seemed bent on puncturing him with needles three times a day.

By mid-December the weather had turned extremely cold, which may have had as much to do with the bear's recovery as anything I was shooting into him. On our second straight zero-degree day, I could get no closer than forty yards from him. To get any kind of a shot, I was going to have to go into the enclosure.

I was banking on the fear reflex that he had learned whenever he saw me with the gun. But if he suddenly realized that I was on his turf, I was in for deep trouble.

Fitzgerald and several other keepers stood by the gate, armed with snatch poles, ready to follow me in and attempt a rescue if necessary. We stamped around in the snow breathing gusts of icy air as I loaded the pistol and slipped two extra darts into the pocket of my jacket. Our faithful band of off-track bettors drifted up.

"You be careful, Mike," John said, "the television news people called this morning. They're going to come down tomorrow and film you shooting the bear. We don't want to spoil their story."

I nodded. John unlocked the heavy gate and I stepped in. The bear, I heard, was getting three-to-one odds among the bettors.

It saw me and hesitated. I waved the gun. He turned and climbed up the mountain. I followed, cursing the slippery footing.

Just as I reached the top, I glanced over and saw him busily climbing down the other side. Whenever I started down, he started up, staying as far away from me as possible. It was like a game; one that he was far better suited to play than I. I began to turn numb in the bitter cold, and decided to try a shot while I could still control the shaking in my hands.

I looked down, judged the distance, and fired. The dart arched through the air and, through sheer luck, struck him perfectly in the rump.

He huffed. A long roll of steam issued from his nostrils. Ignoring the dart, he took the initiative and started up the steep cliff after me. Our goals were suddenly reversed, and it was my turn to play keep-away. Half-sliding, I scrambled down the face of the mountain, raced around the pool, and was out of the gate just as John got it unlocked and partly opened. We got an appreciative round of applause. Probably from the spectators who had taken the long odds.

We repeated this dangerous little charade after lunch, and again just before sundown. But the third time I hit him, he had had enough. Instead of chasing up the mountain after me, he jumped into the empty pool and just sat there.

"I don't think he can get out, Mike!" John yelled.

I carefully descended the cliff and trotted past the pit. The bear glared, but made no attempt to climb out.

Word must have gotten around. The next morning the polar bear enclosure was surrounded by 300 people, five reporters, and three television cameras. John and I answered a number of relevant questions ("What size needle do you use?" "Do you ever miss a shot?" "Do you think we're going to have another Ice Age?") and a few fanciful queries ("What's wrong with the polar bear?").

The bear was still at the bottom of the empty pool, and looked too weak to climb out. Someone suggested that we fill the pool with water, so he could swim out. I was afraid to take the chance. He might be too weak even to swim.

John came up with a better idea. The zoo had a large supply of baled hay on hand to feed the herbivores. We could throw enough bales into the pit to allow him to climb out, then lure him into an adjoining pen while they were removed. It sounded reasonable, and we decided to try it.

"I might as well give him a shot of antibiotics while he's still in there," I said. It wouldn't be nearly as dramatic as the bear and I chasing each other up and down the cliff in front of the television cameras, I realized. But shooting what amounted to a fish in a barrel was a lot safer.

We explained the plan to the reporters. They looked disappointed. But, having set up all their equipment, they decided to film anyway.

It had been snowing steadily all morning. As I entered the pen and approached the pit, I could see the bear curled like a giant ice cube in the corner.

He sensed my presence, stood up, and growled. I hit him with the injection before he could move. I turned and started trudging toward the gate. Halfway there, I noticed a strange, open-mouthed expression on the faces of the people outside the fence. They were all staring over my shoulder. There was only one conceivable reason for that.

Without looking back, I dived for the door. I slid through it, spread-eagled on the ground, and heard it slam shut. An instant later, a giant white apparition hit it. The bear, left to his own devices, had vacated the pit.

Several people helped me to my feet, and as I was brushing off the snow a young lady from a local news program thrust a microphone in my face.

"Is the bear okay now?" she asked.

"It seems able to get around," I said.

"But he must be cold," she continued. "Isn't it cruel not to move him into a nice warm place where he could get well?"

"Lady," I said, "to that bear, this is summer. Now that it's snowing, it's probably the first time he's been happy for a year."

Blushing but unflustered, she turned her attention to the bear and began describing his activities for the camera. And he picked that instant to begin his recovery.

Having narrowly missed a 160-pound veterinarian for lunch, he settled for a dead fish that happened to be lying nearby. It was the first time he had shown any interest in feeding for almost a month.

Fitzgerald cheered. The bear finished his fish in two savage bites and looked around for more. Another keeper was dispatched to get a pail of fresh fish.

For a change, there was a pleasant story—complete with happy ending—on the local news that night.

During the past decade, the concept of zoo design has changed drastically. The newer zoos are being built farther from the clogged urban areas, where a more natural habitat can be simulated. Visitors take a bus or a monorail to see the animals and, for the animals most certainly, it's a big improvement.

The advantage of a smaller, city zoo, is in a closer proximity. Those people who have come to wonder at and appreciate and study the variety of life on our planet are given the chance to see it nearly nose to nose. The disadvantage comes from the minority of thoughtless people who inadvertently injure the animals on exhibit and from an even smaller minority of lunatic fringe people who seem to enjoy this sort of mistreatment.

All manner of debris is thrown into the cages, simply to see how the animals react to it. Junk food, tennis balls, crumpled papers, even hard drugs are fed to the hapless victims.

I have seen the chimpanzees at Central Park careening off the walls in a frenzy after ingesting amphetamines, fed to them by a user with a sadly mistaken sense of humor.

There is little that can be done about such activity. You can't stop and search everyone who comes to a zoo, and all the exhibits can't be watched all of the time. But the incident of this cruel practice rises and falls in direct correlation to the availability of drugs on the street.

The great walrus at the New York Aquarium died because someone fed it a foreign object. Animals are likely to swallow anything thrown to them and can easily develop an intestinal obstruction. If unreported, something like that is difficult to diagnose. The animal will go off its feed for a couple of days, but by the time it is X-rayed, and the obstruction discovered, irreparable damage may have already occurred.

For several years I have been concerned about the rash of television programs that depict people living with nature. Wilderness men romp around a scenic setting, hugging friendly bears, and scratching whole packs of wolves behind their fuzzy ears. It's a potentially dangerous projection of what may be involved when dealing with wild animals. In this case, violence on television may not be as bad as nonviolence on television.

It's certainly nice to show someone caring for animals. But some people have accepted the idea that if they like an animal, it won't hurt them will, in fact, return their warmth.

In 1978 a human leg was found in the polar bear pen at the Prospect Park Zoo. It was never claimed or identified. Someone had obviously just wanted to see what it was like climbing into a bear den at night. In the past, animals that dared attack people who did something like that were summarily shot. Twice in the last decade, polar bears were shot to death by policemen who were attempting to rescue someone who had shoved his arm through the bars and had been grabbed and maimed.

Also in 1978 a child lost his arm in New York, trying to pet a grizzly. He would have been dragged into the pen and killed if a friend hadn't stabbed the bear in the foot with his pocket knife. The bears cannot be blamed. Bears eat small mammals. And people are small mammals.

The gorilla is an endangered species and, with the recent development of West African agriculture, will doubtless become extinct within a very few generations. Zoo breeding of such a species is essential if they are to be saved in any form. New Yorkers are justly proud of our own collection, which includes Congo, a giant and very healthy male.

The vast majority of animals rely on their sense of smell to interpret the world around them. The great apes, like man, rely primarily on sight. They are highly vulnerable to human diseases and, in captivity, to human foibles.

Over a million people passed through the great ape house to see Congo's firstborn daughter, Pattycake. Only one of them made the mistake of exchanging a traditional stick of tobacco with the father.

A man, smoking a cigarette, stopped in front of the cage. He noticed the gorilla watching his actions carefully. On a whim, he flicked the cigarette into the cage.

Congo picked it up and, after mimicking him and taking a few drags, settled back on his haunches. For reasons unknown, the man then reached into the cage to retrieve his smoke. He pulled it out of Congo's mouth.

He lost four fingers.

If there is anything dumber than giving a cigarette to a gorilla, it must be trying to take one away from him.

But because of incidents like this, fences are pulled back, making a wider separation between people and animal. And zoos have started to install plexiglass windows to protect the animals, and more fences beyond the windows. The separation, both in attitude and in actual space, continues to widen.

13
Quintana Roo

It was a quiet November evening. The first snowfall was beginning to accumulate in the streets. I was home alone, reading, perfectly content to spend the rest of the winter in my living room. The phone rang. An emergency, I assumed; an invitation to trudge through the chilly streets and treat an ailing animal. I answered it. And four days later I was trudging through the jungles of the Yucatan to treat an ailing human.

"Mike? It's Elena. You busy?"

I hadn't heard from her for nearly six months, but we always seem to pick up our relationship as though one of us had just stepped out of the room, and our conversations usually start in mid-sentence.

"No, not really. What's up?"

"How would you like to go diving with Jacques Cousteau?"

"Sure," I said, "come on over. I'll fill the tub."

"No kidding, Mike. He's in Yucatan, filming a show on sharks. I talked him into letting us dive with the *Calypso* crew."

I paused. It was a tremendous opportunity, and I had done some diving—but certainly not enough to keep up with the famous French oceanographer. I voiced my doubts to Elena.

"Don't worry," she said, "I told him you've been diving for twenty years."

"You lied? To Jacques Cousteau?"

"Come on, Mike, it'll be fun. But they've already started filming, so you'd better get down here in a hurry." She didn't have long to talk. She had bummed a ride on an air force plane from the Yucatan to Mexico City, just to call me, and had to make her connection back. There was a small airstrip near the village where she worked, but flights in and out were infrequent.

"I have surgery scheduled for tomorrow," I said, "but I think I can get away for a few days after that."

"Great. See you then!" She hung up.

The invitation came as no great surprise. Elena has always been something of a free spirit, far from the image one might have of a professional archaeologist. Although only in her mid-thirties, she had spent most of her adult life in the jungles of Mexico and was currently running an archaeological dig for the Mexican government in the federal territory of Quintana Roo.

She lived alone, directing two hundred men working at the site. It was an unheard-of position for a female. In that remote province of the Yucatan women were considered to be worth next to nothing. She ran the project in a cool-mannered and forceful way, allowing no nonsense. But she always showed up wearing a machete at her belt.

The workers accepted her authority. She obviously knew her business. But not everyone in the province was as impressed. When we eventually found time to sit down and talk, she brought me up to date on her recent adventures. She seemed to enjoy the role of a liberated woman, holding her own in a part of the world that was traditionally male-dominated. I admired her tremendously for this but, in all honesty, I would not have wanted to exchange places with her.

Shortly after taking the job, she was sitting in the village's only restaurant having a drink one evening. A native woman walked in, leveled a gun at her head, and said, "You're the one who's been running around with my husband! Count to five, and then you're gonna die!"

Elena is tall and blonde, quite attractive, and had been the subject of wild rumors ever since her arrival. While the other customers at the bar scrambled to safety, Elena began to talk to the woman, quietly and calmly. It took Elena nearly half an hour to convince the woman that she had, indeed, tried to seduce the incredibly handsome man in question. But being a good husband, he had rejected her. And Elena promised to control her passions and stay away from him in the future.

Pacified, the woman spared her and left.

The worse thing about it, Elena told me, was that she hadn't even liked the guy. He had made a pass at her, and she had brushed him off. Naturally he couldn't go back to his friends and tell them he had been rejected, so his rather lurid tale of conquest had somehow gotten back to his wife.

The dig was a major project. A good many acres of jungle had to be cleared to uncover the remains of what could prove to be another ancient Mayan city.

Working through a rather casual governmental system of red tape, someone had evidently failed to file one set of proper papers with the proper clerk. The property owner felt that his land was being dug up without his permission. He showed up at the dig with a dozen friends. All were on horseback and all carried shotguns.

Elena met them. They were looking for the man in charge, they said, to blow his brains out. She told them that, in fact, she was the man in charge.

They were very upset. There was nothing really wrong with killing a woman but there was no honor in it either. If you came home and said you'd shot a woman, it was better if you hadn't done anything.

She was scared that her male assistant, who had taken a truck into the village for supplies, might show up. They would automatically assume that she had been lying and would probably kill him. Luckily, he was delayed and she talked the owner into a compromise.

On behalf of the Mexican government, she offered to appoint him officially in charge of the archaeological project. On behalf of his government, he could not refuse. He dismounted, poked around a bit, then led his band off into the jungle, standing tall in the saddle.

It took me a couple of days to clear things up at the office, deal with the most pressing cases, and arrange for a flight to the Yucatan. I assumed the environment would be similar to the Brazilian rain forest so I packed the same gear I had taken on the earlier trip, including jungle boots instead of hiking shoes. It was a mistake I was soon to regret.

I changed planes in Mexico City and arrived just as the sun was rising. The village, thirty miles north of the ancient Mayan city of Tulum, was little more than a collection of wooden cabins with thatched roofs, an air strip, and a small restaurant overlooking the sea. It had been built to attract some of the tourists who came to the island of Cozumel just offshore. And a few miles into the jungle was an Indian village.

Elena had left a message for me at the restaurant. She was at the dig and would meet me for dinner that night. Cousteau, unfortunately, had finished filming and was gone. But she had arranged a surprise for me.

She had been telling everyone that I was flying in and had, I fear, somewhat inflated the stories of my ability to cope with the wilderness. That section of Quintana Roo was under the control of a man named Sergio, who was quite interested in her romantically. The more she talked, the more jealous he became. And when she said I would probably want to do some exploring, he saw his chance to expose this gringo. He offered to supply a guide.

I met the guide at the restaurant. He was the toughest, hardest-walking Indian tracker in the territory and Sergio had instructed him to hike me into the ground. Most of the Indians are bilingual, speaking both Spanish and classic Mayan, but he knew a little English too. My Spanish was rusty, so we communicated mostly by sign language. He was short and wiry, about my size, and ready to go.

I checked into my cabin, changed into jungle gear, and had a light breakfast before we left. I was running five to ten miles every day in New York, and was in pretty good shape for a thirty-nine-year-old. He was a bit younger and had spent his life tracking the backwaters of the Yucatan.

He set a rapid pace as we moved out. For awhile it didn't bother me. But the Yucatan peninsula is a lot drier than the Amazon basin and I could feel the rocks beginning to dig through the soles of my soft jungle boots.

The Yucatan is a heavily forested limestone plain under a thin layer of dry soil. The rains, over the centuries, have created a number of natural wells and caverns in the limestone. The Indian wanted to show me one of these caverns, so we took along a flashlight and a battery-powered lantern. He neglected to tell me that the cavern was ten miles distant, half a day's march under the best of conditions.

The underbrush was dense. There are no real seasons in the Yucatan, no chance for plants to fall to the ground and become humus in the winter. Things grow continually. We moved through massive stands of mahogany, and all around us, constantly, the sounds of nature gone wild. A family of coatimundis followed us for more than a mile, capering through the lower branches and along the vague trail behind us. Occasionally there was a break in the canopy of overgrowth and we could see patches of brilliant blue sky and drifting clouds.

The Yucatan is best known for the fabulous archaeological remains of the pre-Columbian Mayan Empire, and most of the scattered inhabitants, known as Yucatec Indians, are direct descendants of the Maya. They were fierce, well-organized, and independent, and might never have been conquered when the Spanish arrived in the sixteenth century, if a special set of circumstances had not existed at the time.

Power struggles within the empire had weakened its structure. Natural disasters—a series of terrible storms that swept across the peninsula—wiped out much of the fertile agricultural areas. Then the Spanish came and the conquest of Mexico began. But the Mayan society was already in such decline that the invaders refused to believe the peoples they found were descended from the builders of Chichen Itza or Mayapan.

The inhabitants of this remote province did not bow lightly to conquest. They won their independence under the leadership of Andres Quintana Roo in 1821. But the territory, though largely still unexplored, is slowly succumbing to western civilization. Railroads, aimed at the rich mahogany forests, are being built. And the coastal climates have attracted the notice of conglomerates which are buying land for the construction of tourist resorts. The inroads of civilization are a bit more subtle than when Cortez first came to Mexico but are no less devastating to a primary culture.

In Brazil the massive jungle itself has served as a buffer. Many tribes in the interior still live in a pristine state. The Yucatan is smaller and more vulnerable. The beautifully beaded shirts and costumes are rapidly giving way to chambray and dungarees. And, especially among the young, the racial memories of a mighty empire seem to fade before the mechanical splendor of a Coca-Cola machine.

Shortly after noon, the guide halted. I was certainly ready for a break but had quickly caught the mood of competition from him and was not about to show my fatigue. He pushed aside some branches, revealing a small opening on the side of a gently rolling hill. He nodded and crawled in on his hands and knees. I followed.

An underground stream trickled through the passageway, soaking our pants and sleeves. The light behind us faded. A hundred yards into the sloping corridor, he stood up and clicked on the lantern.

Before us spread the inky surface of an undisturbed, underground lake. He hoisted the lantern over his head. Delicate limestone stalactites hung from the ceiling like jeweled pendants. I began to tremble. The temperature in the cavern was thirty to forty degrees lower than on the surface.

I have toured a number of North American caves, where the natural beauty of the formations has been enhanced by artifical lights. I had always wondered what they must have looked like to the first explorers. The guide turned off the lantern.

For a moment we were in utter, absolute, darkness. It was the day before Creation.

Moments passed. Then I must have made some sound, some unconscious vocalization to prove my existence, if nothing else.

The light reappeared. The guide was grinning.

We never reached, or could even make out, the farthest depths of the cavern. We drank of the water—beautiful, pure, and icy—and he caught a cave fish which we roasted for lunch. It was one of the blind, mutant species found only in such caves, or at great depths in the seas, where light is totally diffused.

We started back, taking another route. I must have appeared still too chipper to him, because we crossed rocky hillocks, doubled back, and always seemed to hit the densest undergrowth.

Late that afternoon, after hiking for nearly twelve hours, we hit the rutted road that lead to the village. My legs started feeling rubbery. He was still moving fast but had been unusually quiet for the past hour. I glanced over at him. His jaws were tense, his lips pursed, and his legs just weren't moving as straight and smooth as they had been.

I began to slow down. He stopped, a look of grim triumph in his eyes. We stood there a minute, both grimy, sweaty, and beyond exhaustion.

"Usted es un hombre magnifico," I said, in my best high school Spanish, then broke into English, "but let's call the whole thing off."

The last mile was like a casual stroll through the park, for both of us. We had already passed the village where he lived. He offered to take me back and introduce me to his family. I declined. I had to meet Elena for dinner. He wanted to know how long I would be in Quintana Roo. I was leaving shortly, I said. He indicated that, before I left, I should spend an evening exploring that particular stretch of the road. Some interesting creatures, he assured me, only come out after the sun has gone down.

"Tequila, por favor."

The bartender poured me a shot, and I tossed it down with lime and salt. It hit bottom like a rock, and I began to relax. Normally I don't drink hard liquor, especially on an empty stomach. But in Rome I drink what the Romans drink.

It was nearly eight o'clock. I had barely had time to shower and change before meeting Elena for dinner. She was late, so I had a drink and tried to shake off some of the exhaustion.

A rather tall, well-dressed Mexican joined me at the bar. "Another of the same, for both of us," he said, "and make it a double."

I smiled and nodded. We drank in silence. And to be polite, I ordered a round.

Although I didn't know it at the time, this was Sergio, the local straw boss, who had arranged for my guide on the hike. He must have figured out who I was and been surprised that I had made it back at all.

We chatted. The weather. How did I like the Yucatan? Had I seen the interior? How long was I staying? He ordered another round. There is more than one way to skin a gringo. Even though Elena had assured him that our relationship had always been platonic, he would have prefered me dead, drunk, or both.

I should have known better than to get into the game of macho with him, but the third round of double shots went down a good deal easier. And by the fourth, of course, the pride of the Yankees was at stake.

By nine o'clock the room had taken on a jaunty tilt, and my legs had gone rubbery (again). But my feet were no longer sore. In fact, there was no feeling in them at all. To maintain any semblance of sobriety, I was backed up against the bar, leaning on my elbows, so I could hold the glass steady. Sergio stood beside me, quite casually, with one arm propped on the bar. He was into a long, rambling story about his childhood in Veracruz, and I was trying to remember exactly why I was in this place at this particular time.

Elena walked in, wearing boots, breeches, and a work shirt. She had just gotten back from the dig and had hurried straight over. "You've met!" she said, delighted, then kissed us both.

"Another round!" said Sergio.

Elena began talking immediately. She apologized for my having missed Cousteau, said she would take me diving the next day, and announced she was starving.

Sergio walked an incredibly straight line to the table and sat down. I followed, slowly and carefully, and Elena brought up the rear.

Sergio and I were extremely polite. We were impressed with each other's capacity for the raw liquor and both determined not to pass out in front of Elena.

"What would you like for dinner?" he asked.

"Are there any Peruvian lobsters around?" I said.

"Certainly!" He clapped his hands. Three men who had been drinking at the end of the bar, hustled over to our table. He mumbled something to them and they took off. Then he turned to us. "We'll have another drink. The lobsters will take a little while."

"I'll have something else, if it's any trouble," I said.

Sergio glared stiffly. "The gringo wants lobster. My divers have gone to capture them."

Curtly, I nodded.

For the first time since she walked in, Elena looked at us closely. "You are both drunk," she concluded.

"I am not drunk," said Sergio.

"And I am just as not drunk as he is," I said.

She began to laugh at our pathetic poses. "I see," she said. "Well, now that we've all proven our manhood by getting pissy-eyed, let's have dinner." Elena has a talent for getting directly to the point. And her laughter is highly contagious.

The lobsters were delicious, when they finally arrived. And halfway through dinner, I told Elena and Sergio about this crazy guide who had tried to hike me to a frazzle. Sergio topped the story, of course, by admitting that it was his idea.

Early the next morning, Elena came by the cabin to pick me up. It was a beautiful Sunday morning, the back of her jeep was full of skin-diving equipment, and I hovered near death with a tequila hangover.

"When is the next plane out of here?" I said. "I want to get up to about ten thousand feet and jump out."

"Tomorrow. And nobody told you to swill down all that rotgut."

"Where's Sergio?"

"Not up yet. I don't think he's going along. He has two armed guards posted outside the door."

Miguel, one of Sergio's divers, went along with us. We drove toward the beach. The bumpy, rutted road did very little to improve my health.

"There are some underwater caves about a mile up the coast," Elena said, swerving to hit a small boulder.

"Maybe we can find the sharks that Cousteau was filming."

"What's so special about them?"

"There's this thing about sharks. Supposedly, they've got to swim constantly, throughout their lives, or else they die. But he found some that were sleeping. Or hibernating, or something."

I grunted.

"You'll feel better after a dip," she said. "Then we'll go back and have some breakfast."

She pulled over and we got out. We were on top of a cliff. Twenty feet below us the barest sliver of a beach sloped into a deep green lagoon. There seemed to be no path leading down to the beach.

They started getting into their flippers, masks, and tanks and I followed suit. Miguel walked over, stepped off the cliff, and disappeared. Before I could say anything, Elena waved cheerfully and jumped in after him.

My idea of diving had always been to climb over the side of a boat, then swim down to deeper water. But anyone who would start their dive off a twenty-foot cliff, with all that equipment strapped on them, would have to be crazy. But there was no other way down. So I jumped.

But instead of going in feet first, as they had done, I automatically arched forward into a standard lifesaving jump, leaning slightly forward with arms extended. A second later, I learned why sky-divers usually straighten up before opening their chutes. I had not strapped the tank onto my back tightly enough. Just as I hit the water, the tank hit me in the back of the head.

I couldn't have blacked out for more than a few seconds, but when I opened my eyes I was completely disoriented. All I knew was that my head hurt, my lungs hurt, I couldn't breathe, and fish seemed to be swimming around in the air.

As my head cleared, I grabbed the mouthpiece, flushed it with the valve, took several deep breaths from the tank, and surfaced.

They were bobbing around, waiting for me. I pointed to my head, then to the beach, and swam toward it. I needed to sit down, very quietly, somewhere.

When the pain had subsided, I gingerly entered the water and swam down to join them. They were hovering near the cliff, about twenty-five feet below the surface. They had, indeed, found an underwater cavern. The entrance was about three feet wide and Miguel was inspecting it with his light. Finally, he swam in and we followed. The tide was more noticeable in the narrow shelf, eaten from the limestone by the sea. It was murky, a good deal of silt had drifted in and settled, and the feeling of claustrophobia was immediate.

Thirty yards in, it became too narrow to continue. There were no sharks, no fish, nothing. It seemed odd. As we neared the entrance again we saw the reason. On the way in we had unknowingly passed the crevass of a full-grown moray eel. He had come out to protect his territory.

A five-foot moray, like this one was, can be dangerous. They have large, powerful teeth, a gaping mouth, and will attack anything that moves when they feel threatened.

With an unlimited supply of air we could have just sat back and waited for him to go away. But the tanks were running low; we would either have to make a break for it or simply drown. We began edging along the wall. Miguel kept trying to distract him with the light, but twice he lunged at us, and we froze. Luckily, there were three of us—more than he was willing to take on at the moment. After each lunge he retreated nearer and nearer to his den. Warily, he backed in. Very slowly, so as not to upset him, we edged out one by one.

Elena and I spent the rest of the day, as we always do when our paths happen to cross, just sitting around talking. She is an active woman in an interesting field that has taken her to the most remote parts of Mexico and Central America. But she was worried about the general feel of things among the nationals. Resentment against Americans was running high and the government seemed less and less inclined to cooperate. (Three months later, she lost her job in the Yucatan, and had to return to the States. Sergio quit his own job in protest of this treatment—quite a rare and noble gesture, considering the status of women in Mexico.)

Sergio joined us for dinner, then excused himself. He still looked under the weather and I wasn't in much better shape. But I was leaving the next day and wanted to see as much as possible, so I asked Elena to show me the Indian village.

"Fine," she said, "they've heard all about you."

"I hope there are no more jealous lovers."

"Don't worry. A couple of the men are in my work crew, but they keep pretty much to themselves."

I picked up my camera at the cabin, we climbed in the jeep, and started out the road I had taken on my hike.

The sun had just gone down. She turned on the headlights and immediately hit the brakes.

We sat in absolute silence. And I remembered what my hiking guide had said. Some interesting creatures come out at night.

For as far as we could see, the road was covered with tarantulas. Big ones. Tarantulas that made my pet at home look like a runt. Hundreds of them had crawled out to soak up the last warmth of the sun retained by the road. Slowly and majestically they moved about, completely ignoring the jeep. For many of us it would be the raw material for a lifetime of nightmares.

"Do they come out like this every night?" I asked Elena.

"No. Not in this region, anyway. I think it has something to do with the weather."

I didn't know much about tarantulas at that time, but I did want some photographs. And right beside me sat an expert photographer. Elena had had work in any number of journals, plus an exhibition of her photos on Long Island. Anthropologist. Archaeologist. Photographer. She was everything except gullible.

So I tried buttering her up. Weren't we lucky to have this great camera equipment along? And, I wouldn't trust anyone in the world to handle it, except her, of course. And, I was all right on long shots, but my close-ups usually turned out blurry and amateurish. And, she took the camera and got out of the jeep.

A tarantula the size of a pumpkin pie had settled on the road just ahead of us. Elena got down on her hands and knees and started snapping.

"Move in a little closer," I said, "and see if you can

flip him over on his back to catch the underside."

By then she was completely engrossed in the job. She grabbed a stick, flipped the spider over, and continued firing.

Suddenly she stopped, realized what she was doing, and jumped to her feet. "I've been had!" she yelled. "You conned me into this, you skunk!"

She scrambled back into the jeep, jammed it in gear, and started making a slow detour around the spider convention. But she refused to speak to me.

Finally, I said, "It wouldn't have hurt you. They never attack people."

Silence a moment, then, "Are you sure?"

"Pretty sure," I said.

We got back on the road and within minutes could see the flickering lights of the Indian village in the distance. Suddenly a native appeared in the headlights, waving his arms. We pulled up.

Excitedly, he pointed at me and asked her, "Es el medico?"

Elena nodded.

I didn't catch his next few sentences, but Elena kept nodding, and he crawled in the back. We took off.

"Someone's been hurt in the village," she said.

"Isn't there a doctor here?"

"There's one at the resort, out on Cozumel. It would take two days to get him here. A kid hurt his foot badly, and they know my friend, the doctor, is in town."

"Didn't you tell them I'm a vet?"

She shrugged. "Doctors are doctors."

The village was a collection of wooden huts, surrounding a clearing. A few kerosene lamps provided the only light, and perhaps two dozen Indians were gathered around a figure on the ground.

Some of the Indians came to greet us. They all had the high cheekbones and narrow features of the classic Mayan, and the basic distrust of outsiders common to all oppressed groups.

The injured boy looked to be in his late teens. He was laying quietly on a makeshift wooden platform, very stoically, not saying a word. But he was sweating, and I could see the pain in his eyes.

Half the length of an eight-inch railroad spike was buried in the heel of his right foot.

Elena asked them how it had happened, then translated for me. He had jumped out of a tree and landed directly on the spike, hidden in the undergrowth. It had entered his foot at an angle and bent.

"Have them build a bonfire," I said. "There's really not enough light to see anything."

I had a few tetracycline pills in my pocket. But these antibiotics and my pocketknife were all I had to work with. "I don't suppose they have a first-aid kit, or anything like that?"

Elena spoke to the village leader. He came up with a pair of pliers, a syringe, and some local anesthetic left them by a missionary. The syringe, an old-fashioned glass and metal affair, was rusty. The anesthetic, procaine, had turned yellow with age.

After the bonfire was going, I asked them to boil some water. I scraped the rust off the syringe and needle, and put it in to boil along with my pocketknife. I asked for some alcohol to sterilize everything with. They brought me a bottle of homemade tequila.

Twenty minutes later, I fished the syringe and knife from the boiling water, poured tequila over them, and set them on fire. The alcohol burned off. They were as sterile as they were ever going to be. I gave the boy a healthy slug of tequila and took one myself. Then I injected the procaine and prepared to remove the spike.

Everyone in the village crowded around to watch, except the boy's father. Throughout the operation, he shuffled around the circle, mumbling and chanting to himself.

I touched the spike gently. The boy nearly fainted from the pain. It occurred to me that if the boy passed out, the natives might think I had killed him. And I had no idea what their reaction would be to that. But if I didn't remove the spike, he would certainly die from tetanus or loss of blood.

I gave him another drink of tequila. We had no common language but I tried to assure him by the tone of my voice. Four of the largest village men were instructed to hold him down.

I began cutting around the spike, trying to loosen it. It was in at an angle and there was no way to remove it without damaging a lot of the surrounding tissue.

The boy screamed.

I worked the spike out as rapidly as possible with the pliers.

The boy's eyes rolled back as blood began to bubble from the wound. I let it bleed a minute, to flush out the area, then finished up. When he regained consciousness, I gave him the tetracycline pills.

"They really ought to take him out to the doctor," I said, getting to my feet.

"He's a gringo," said Elena, "they don't trust him."

The boy's father had stopped his dancing and chanting. He came up and hugged me, expressing his thanks.

I turned around and saw a whole line of Indians with ailments waiting for treatment. A child with scurvy. A little girl with boils. A woman with an eye infection. And all I had with me was my pocketknife.

I did the best I could with it. I explained basic hygienic treatment for each case and had Elena translate. There wasn't much I could do about the scurvy. You would think that in such a paradise they could grow a wide variety of fruits, but the topsoil is thin and after a single season of planting and harvesting the fields turn to sand.

We left the village shortly after midnight. Four hours had passed and my head was swirling. As the jeep rumbled along through the jungle, I asked Elena, "What was that fellow chanting about? The one who hugged me."

"He was making up a song. To drive off evil spirits, or something. And to assure them that, if the gringo doctor killed his son, he would kill the gringo doctor."

"Why didn't you tell me?"

"I was nervous enough for both of us," she said. "Besides, he wouldn't have killed you."

"Are you sure?"

"Pretty sure," she said.

14
Roundup Time in Flushing

The zoo in Flushing Meadows is the most modern of the three New York City animal facilities. It was designed and built to incorporate much of the natural landscape, to get away from the idea of a zoo being a prison for wild things. All the animals are safely enclosed, primarily to protect them from the people. But there is no such thing as a maximum security zoo.

Three times in the past five years animals have escaped from the Flushing Zoo. On each occasion tracking them through the suburban streets and recapturing them was much more a comedy of errors than a menace to the public. And as the city zoo vet, I was called upon to direct the roundup to minimize injury to the animals.

I had been invited to a Passover dinner in April, 1975.

It was a Wednesday, my usual day for making the rounds at the zoos, but things were quiet. The only scheduled case was a whitetail deer in Flushing. It had an infected molar, which I wanted to remove. The zoo was on the way to my dinner engagement, so before leaving, I changed into a brand new charcoal gray suit, then drove out.

The zoo attendants had already isolated the deer, and I had no trouble anesthetizing it and performing the oral surgery. But just as I was getting back into my coat, a man came over to the fence and said, "Say, did you fellows lose a deer? There's one wandering around over on the golf course."

Just to be safe we counted the herd. And came up one short. I reloaded my tranquilizer pistol, and five of us headed for the nearby golf course.

In the distance we heard someone yell, "Hey! There goes a moose!" We broke into a run.

We cleared a rise and came upon two very shaken people, both pointing in different directions, both babbling about how they had just been attacked by a strange creature. I realized that as the word spread the police would be inundated by reports of people spotting deer. Or worse. People would see exactly what they wanted to see. For some, the long-awaited invasion from outer space was at hand.

April is not the ideal time of year to go sloshing through a golf course in Flushing, no matter how you are dressed. There is poor footing on the fairways, the greens are brown, and the roughs impassable. After fifteen minutes of slipping, sliding, and searching fruitlessly, we were all filthy.

We spotted a car, parked on the road that surrounds the course. The motor was running, the doors were open, the keys still in it. One of the zoo keepers coming back from lunch had spotted the deer swimming across a pond. He had abandoned his car and gone after it.

We later learned that he had waded through the pond and, dripping wet, approached an elderly woman and asked for a dime to make a phone call. He wanted to call the office to alert them.

"Take the money!" she yelled, throwing her purse on the ground. "Just don't hurt me!"

His rather improbable explanation failed to convince her, he said. But he did take a dime, located a pay phone, and found all the lines busy. When he came back to return the dime, she had vanished.

We locked up his car and took the keys with us. We were mud-splattered and out of breath. I was carrying the pistol. I suppose we must have looked like fugitives from a chain gang; people began avoiding us. One brave soul pointed at a distant construction site before making a hasty departure. We climbed a fence and headed for the site. When we got there, it seemed deserted. We spread out and began searching around the cranes and other heavy equipment.

Suddenly the deer appeared. He came charging straight at me from behind a bulldozer. I leveled the gun, aiming at his chest. Then it occured to me that, even if I hit him with the tranquilizer dart, he was going to keep on running for ten minutes. And the first place he was going to run was over me. He was not the world's largest whitetail buck, but he was moving rapidly and in a straight line.

I dived into a sand dune. The deer thundered by.

"Why didn't you shoot him?" someone yelled.

The panicky animal clattered across a road and into a cemetery. It was Easter week and a good many people were there to pay their respects to the departed. We followed the shouts.

I climbed on top of a large tombstone to get a better view and spotted the deer moving toward the far fence. A woman, changing the flowers at a nearby grave, looked startled.

"It's okay, lady," I said. "I'm looking for my deer."

"Do you plan on shooting her?" she asked, nodding toward my pistol.

"She escaped from the zoo," I explained and hopped down. I motioned to my cohorts and the Dalton Gang resumed the chase.

Finally, we cornered it. And just as I got within shooting range, it sailed over the fence and onto the Van Wyck Expressway. Cars began to swerve. Some motorists pulled over, some sped by. The deer raced up the highway in the direction of traffic. I started over, wondering if perhaps there wasn't room in the *Guinness Book of Records* for fences climbed in a three-hour period.

One of the keepers headed back for the car we had locked. It was obvious that we weren't going to be able to keep up with the deer on foot.

We trotted along beside the road, trying to keep the animal in sight. Before we had gone a hundred yards, we heard a siren behind us. We stopped and turned around. A highway patrolman pulled up behind us. The officer stepped out of his car, and stood shielded behind the open door.

"Put down the gun," he said.

The barrel of his police special was aimed just south of my shoulders. Carefully, I placed the tranquilizer pistol on the ground in front of me and raised my hands.

Judging from the look on his face, we would have to come up with an extremely rational explanation for the situation. And if the park employees had not been in uniform, and carrying identification, I'm sure we would have wound up in Bellevue.

As it was, the cop joined the chase. We all piled into the police car, he turned on the siren, and we were off. Two miles up the road, one of the keepers spotted the deer disappearing into a housing development. We got out at the next exit, turned back, and followed the crowds.

The deer was in someone's back yard, and a mob of people had surrounded the area. I shoved my way through and tranquilized the deer. One of the keepers called the zoo for a van, and the big flap was over.

Being four hours overdue at the party, I didn't bother going home to change my tattered clothing. I may have been late for Passover, but at least I was the first arrival for Halloween.

Two years later, I started dating Sarina Wasserman, who eventually toured the Everglades with me. We had been going out, mostly to shows and museums. One wintry Saturday morning she called me at the office and said, "See if you can think of something different this afternoon. Something besides eighteen museums and a quick lunch."

I said I'd work on it, knowing that with reasonable

luck, something would come up. Considering my profession, I've found that all I have to do is sit down and relax for a quiet afternoon, and within twenty-four hours I'll be wishing things were dull again.

And sure enough, I got a call from the Central Park Zoo. The black panther was sick. What could be more exciting than introducing Sarina to a black panther, while I took blood samples and checked it over? I called her back, she met me, and we drove up to Central Park in a borrowed Mercedes. Before we could get out of the car, Fitzgerald ran up, looking very upset.

"Why aren't you out at Flushing?" he asked.

"Flushing? I came up to treat the black panther."

"That can wait," he said, "the deer are loose, and running all over Queens."

I told him to call the police and see if he could get me an escort, so I wouldn't be stopped for speeding on my way out there. I figured the police would spot a 450 SL Mercedes easily enough and pick me up. We roared off.

At the bridge, I tossed a handful of change in the general direction of the toll basket, and as I geared up, saw at least a dozen other Mercedes 450s on the entrance ramp. The escort missed us, but the traffic lights seemed to be in our favor. At least we weren't stopped. Most of the police cars in the borough of Queens were already at the Flushing Zoo.

We arrived, and I was quickly filled in as to what had happened. It is against the law to take pets into the zoo. But someone had wandered in with their dog. It had become excited by the presence of all these other animals, jumped a fence, and terrified the deer. Whitetails are skittish creatures. The herd panicked, ran through a fence, and escaped.

Surprisingly enough, we found it easier to round up a whole herd of them than it had been to catch an individual. Instinct probably kept them together in this strange, outside environment. Unfortunately, one buck broke from the herd and got onto Queens Boulevard. A team of policemen chased and caught it before it could run afoul of the traffic. But, as sometimes happens with a high-strung creature, it died of shock.

Driving back to Manhattan late that afternoon, Sarina suggested that, on our next date, we do something dull. A visit to the Museum of Natural History, she said, might be nice.

New fences, higher and stronger, were installed at the zoo. They were high enough and strong enough to keep the deer penned in. But they were not constructed to withstand the attack of a powerful natural predator like the timber wolf.

The wolf enclosure at the Flushing Zoo is beautiful. The animals have a large field to roam about in, crossed by a free-flowing stream. There are several dens, and the pack has thrived in this natural setting, growing to fifteen in number. When the first few were aquired, they were pure timber wolves. But other species were donated, primarily by people who had unsuccessfully tried to raise them as pets, and they had interbred.

Although there is no documented record of a healthy person in North America ever being killed by a wolf, they are not just big dogs. Attempts to domesticate them invariably fail. The wolves of Flushing had never killed a living thing. They were well fed and well cared for.

But the instinct was still there, and it erupted the day they escaped.

They are intelligent animals, good parents, and mate for life. But their social structure is very strict. The largest and most aggressive male is the leader of the pack and remains so until he is overthrown. Leadership of this pack had changed only once since I became the zoo veterinarian. I, inadvertently, had caused it.

Two years ago it became necessary to operate on the leader. The last thing he saw, as the absolute leader, was me pointing a tranquilizer gun at him. When he was returned to the enclosure, the younger wolves ganged up on him, and he lost his position. And since then, whenever I am at the zoo, he stalks me. His eyes never leave me. It is, unmistakably, possible for a wolf to hate an individual human being.

The call came in late one fall afternoon. The wolves had somehow dug under their sturdy fence and were loose. Their hunting instinct had surfaced immediately. They crashed into the deer pen, and attacked these natural prey. Flushing Meadows was full of wounded deer being pursued by a pack of baying wolves.

Driving out to Queens, I couldn't help but think of what might happen if, during the chase, I encountered the ex-leader. On equal ground, with no fence to separate us, he would have a golden opportunity to exact payment for the debt I owed him.

The scene was chaos when I pulled up at the administration building. Policemen, armed with shotguns, were ready to spread out through the park. The A.S.P.C.A. had sent a van and a record player. They had decided that we could attract the wolves back into the area by broadcasting a recording of baying dogs over a loud-speaker. It was nearly sundown, the animals had scattered, and the record was going full blast when I arrived.

It was an interesting idea, but I convinced them to shut it off. A wolf will respond to a howling dog about as often as an eagle heeds the mating call of a sparrow.

The police were grim looking. They had seen what the wolves had done in the deer pen and assumed that they were man-killers. Most western wolflore, unfortunately enough, comes from the romantic novels of Jack London or from books written long before the animal was truly understood. I asked them to rack their shotguns and arm themselves with tranquilizer pistols. Half a dozen were kept at the zoo, and I had brought my whole arsenal with me. They looked dubious.

"It's nearly dark," I said, "and there are people around. I don't want to be in the area, chasing wolves, with bullets flying in every direction."

It made sense. I gave them a three-minute course in loading and firing a tranquilizer gun, then we checked out the damage done.

Three of the larger males—including, thank goodness, the ex-leader—had made early kills. They had dragged the bloody whitetail deer carcasses back to their home territory, the wolf enclosure. Their escape tunnel was blocked off, and we were left with the job of rounding up a dozen wolves and what remained of the deer herd.

Most of them had disappeared into the old World's Fair grounds, a large area covering about a hundred acres of land, hills, streams, abandoned pavilions, and winding roads. The rest of the night became a series of near misses and occasional captures, outlined in the glaring headlights of police cars.

The temperature dropped thirty degrees. Police cars and vans raced everywhere. An animal would be spotted, the car would screech to a halt, and people would pour out to run it down on foot.

I spotted a deer being attacked by two wolves on a small island in a gully. We stopped the car, threw a rope over a tree branch, and I swung down into the middle of the scene. I hadn't thought about the wolves' possible reaction to being disturbed in the middle of a kill. I charged them, yelling, "Shoo! Beat it!" Startled, they scampered off down the stream and were picked off by policemen, while I pumped the deer full of painkiller and antibiotics.

We had left the gate to the deer enclosure open, and most of them were herded back in during the first two hours. But the wolf pack had split up and had to be captured individually.

At four in the morning, we were circling Shea Stadium when a wolf calmly stepped into our headlights. I had a snatch pole and was hanging half out the window as we drove after it across the broad parking lot. With a lasso on one end and a spring mechanism on the other, the pole was perfect for capturing an animal in an enclosed area.

The policeman at the wheel hit the gas. "I'll drive up beside him," he yelled, "and you throw on the noose!"

"It's not gonna work," I said.

"Sure it will!"

The wolf was loping along on a straight path.

"Have you ever seen "Wild Kingdom," on television?" I asked the driver.

"How did you know?" he said. He was really excited and getting into the chase.

The gray wolf, running easily, flicked in and out of our lights. But we were gaining on it.

"I just had a feeling you watched it," I said, straining out the window. The lasso was a foot from the wolf's head.

The wolf looked over his shoulder, saw the car, glanced at the rope, then casually cleared a six-foot fence and ran off across a field.

We skidded to a halt.

There aren't any fences on "Wild Kingdom."

By the time the sun was coming up over Long Island, we had managed to capture eleven of the renegades. The final one had been hit by a tranquilizer and had crawled into an abandoned concession stand. He was holed up, ready to take on all comers, but was getting shaky.

We were all tired and anxious to bring an end to the whole thing. I crawled in and grabbed him by one leg and the scruff of the neck. He snapped and struggled, but I was able to avoid the teeth. I dragged him out, and he collapsed.

Six deer had died from wounds or shock. Two automobiles had been demolished in the melee. There were no human casualties, other than those of embarrassment and fatigue.

Fifteen minutes after leaving the scene, I hit the morning traffic, headed for Manhattan. Edging along in my car, it took awhile to readjust emotionally to this most urban of situations. I turned on the radio and learned that the wolves had escaped from the Flushing Zoo last night.

15
Snips and Snails

We do not normally keep timber wolves or even herds of deer at our office on Murray Hill, but we have had our share of both grand and narrow escapes. The difference is, the escapees are almost always humans; clients or innocent bystanders who react adversely to the parade of exotic and sometimes dangerous animals that passes through our door. And there have been times when I wouldn't have minded joining the mass migration myself.

A man once called seeking advice on the treatment of his lizard. It wasn't eating, he said, and was growing progressively listless. I asked him to make an appointment with my secretary, and he brought it in the following day.

With the help of three burly friends, he entered the waiting room carrying what looked like a coffin. It was six feet long, a yard deep, and just narrow enough to fit through the door.

I happened to be in the outer office at the time. "You must be the man with the lizard," I said.

"How did you know? Most people think it's Uncle Charlie."

"You said he was off his feed. What is it, a monitor?"

"Yes. A Komodo dragon."

The coffin rattled. Our other clients began looking nervous. But a couple of spaniel puppies, in for shots, weren't nervous at all. They had picked up a strange scent and were trying to get at the lizard.

The man advised the clients to hold off their dogs. A Komodo dragon, even a half-grown 150-pounder like this one, is a nasty customer. They live primarily on carrion but have been known to attack and kill almost anything that moves, including people and other Komodo dragons. Not the kind of pet you would put on a leash and take out for a morning stroll.

He decided that he wanted out of the box and began lurching around. The men carrying it staggered. Our other clients fled.

Bill and I helped them wrestle the box into the examination room. While everyone held it down, I looked it over and ran some tests. It was a beautiful gray green specimen, the underside splotched with yellow. It measured nearly six feet from nose to tip of tail, and could easily double in size and weight if properly cared for.

It moved quite rapidly for so large a beast, and the examination was a struggle. No one could go near the large and powerful jaws except the owner, and even he was careful.

I suggested he let the meat rot a little longer before feeding, to ease digestion, and wrote him out a prescription. They carried the box out through our deserted waiting room. I told the owner that if he had any problems with it in the future, I'd be glad to make a house call.

Although we try to keep our office menagerie under reasonable control, they are a freewheeling lot and do not always take kindly to visitors. During the year we had him, our cat named Subway seemed to delight in terrorizing people. He was absolutely fearless and became something of an office legend the day he led the attack on the Internal Revenue Service.

He was a completely average-looking brown tabby that one of our clients found in the Fourty-second Street subway terminal and brought in. Subway quickly made friends with the staff and the other animals, but none of our clients could control him. It made finding a home for him something of a problem.

Spotting an unfamiliar lap in the waiting room, he would often leap up in it and quietly accept the petting and fondling of the flattered and unsuspecting client. But when it came time for him to be moved, he would summarily bite the hand that fed his needs. The trapped client would have to wait until a member of the staff could be summoned to remove the creature.

A young girl brought her dog in for an examination before school one morning. While she was waiting, Subway jumped up and settled on her stack of school books.

The girl was told that we would have to keep her dog overnight, and she nodded and prepared to leave. It was a busy day, and no one paid any attention to Subway's whereabouts. Pet owners came in, their animals were treated, and they left.

An hour later, Dr. Woods noticed that the girl was still sitting there and said, "Aren't you late for school?"

Nearly in tears, the girl blurted out, "Subway won't give me my books!"

Dr. Woods chased Subway into the back office, but such incidents kept occuring. Nothing we could do would change his personality. Seemingly, he had found his calling. He was an intimidator.

Then a young couple adopted him. They were familiar with his quirks, had seen him in action, and admired his—for lack of a better word—individuality. I recently had a letter from them, and they think he's the greatest cat in the world. Even though the man has to keep a shaving kit in the office (in case Subway decides to nap in the middle of their bathroom) and they sometimes have to sleep on the living room couch (in case Subway wants to spend the night in the middle of the bedroom).

When the I.R.S. sent an agent in to audit the books, Subway and our other office pets reacted as though it was an invasion of their own private territory. The agent, a cultured and intelligent young woman, was new to the job. She had been well trained and had assisted on a number of audits, but this was her first solo assignment. We set up the auxiliary surgery room for her, moved in a desk, and she began work.

Subway materialized, leaped up onto the desk, and settled in the middle of her papers. I happened to be walking by just at that moment. I picked him up and scooted him away. I offered to close the door.

"No thanks, it's kind of warm in here," she said, "and I like animals."

Within the next two hours, she would drastically revise her humanitarian attitude.

Barnaby, who had a keen nose and a weakness for corned beef, wheeled into the room and went straight for her lunch bag. Moments later, to the vast amusement of our clients, he appeared in the waiting room. Like any shaggy-collared worker, he carried his lunch in a brown paper bag, which he proceeded to demolish. He had always seemed to act as though this was his office, and any food in it was subject to his appetite.

I offered to take the agent to lunch to make up for Barnaby's ill manners. She must have thought my motives included bribery; she declined and went back to work.

Minutes later, Stanley (head honcho among our cats) walked into her room. He was on his way to the water faucet in the sink to knock it open with his paw and get a drink. He stopped to sharpen his claws on her coat, which was draped across a chair.

Then Subway returned to the attack. He curled up on her briefcase and fell asleep. When she needed something out of it and reached down, he bit her.

"Bad cat!" she said.

He bit her again.

We rescued her. She was annoyed. Someone had obviously taught these animals to attack representatives of the government. When she returned to the room, after I had treated her punctured hand, she found blind Arnold standing in the middle of her paperwork. This cat had cystitis, a chronic bladder infection. Whenever he was upset, he urinated. And blind Arnold was upset.

Our apologies didn't seem to help. We cleaned up the mess for her. She was nearing the end of the audit and savagely went back to it.

Fifteen minutes later, her screams brought the whole staff racing toward her room. I was sure that the whole menagerie had attacked her at the same time and was in the process of ripping her to pieces.

Far from it. My sheep dog, in a very un-Barnaby-like moment of weakness, had been seized by an uncontrollable sexual attraction for the agent's leg. He had straddled her knee, while his pelvis made vague thrusting movements, aimed generally at her shin.

Almost every owner of a male dog has faced a similar situation. And while it is perhaps the ultimate gesture of friendship from a canine, it is also an embarrassment.

Quickly, I pulled him off. But the auditor had passed from a mood of steaming indignation into abject fear. She ran for the waiting room, grabbed up the phone, and called her husband.

"Fred," she said, her voice wavering, "you've got to get me out of here. I'm through with this job. A dog stole my lunch, then tried to rape me. A blind cat wet on my papers. Another one bit me. It's a plot."

She paused a moment, listening, then continued. "No," she said, "I'm not hysterical. No, I have not been drinking. Will you please come and get me!"

She insisted on waiting for her husband out on the curb rather than in the office. We brought her things out to her, and she refused to utter another word.

There is controversy regarding the docking of the tails of various breeds of dogs. Some groups feel it is downright cruelty. It is still practiced, primarily on some breeds of show dogs.

Poodle puppies usually are docked at the age of about three days. The bones are still soft, and it's a simple operation. The pup doesn't seem to know what's going on and goes back to nursing at the mother immediately afterward.

A woman recently brought her poodle in for docking. But it was already six months old and at that age, docking is a real operation. The animal must be put under general anesthesia and go through surgery. We explained this to her, and she said to go ahead. She wanted to enter it in dog shows. We measured it and docked half the tail, the normal procedure for poodles.

The next day she returned with the dog and said, "It's too long. Take off another inch."

I told her that it might, at the moment, look a little bit funny to her because the tail had been shaved and was bandaged. She insisted on another inch. We took the dog in and prepared it for surgery. But before I could get around to the operation, she called the office. She wanted an inch and a half taken off, instead of an inch.

We docked it again, to her latest specifications. And ever since, we have all been kind of waiting around for the woman to come back in and ask us to put the inch and a half back on.

The distance afforded by Alexander Graham Bell's invention does not always lend enchantment. People can sometimes say things over the phone that they would be unable to express in person. I have had whispered calls to please hurry over and intercede when pets have become the focal point of marital arguments, to please call the neighbors and tell them to quit upsetting a cat, and once to assure a client that he was not going insane.

The man, who had been a client of mine in Brooklyn, insisted on speaking to me. Sharon called me from the back and I listened to his story.

It had started, he said, with hallucinations. He had seen "things" growing on the trees in his back yard. Repulsive-looking things that seemed to slide along the branches and to grow at an incredible rate.

He always kept his dog penned in the backyard while he was at work and had come home to find one of the creatures dropping off the dog. He had inspected the dog and found some sort of a bite. He wanted to bring the dog in.

He was sure that, after devouring his dog, the things were going to start on him.

We set up an appointment and he brought his animal in. There were a couple of minor wounds that looked like insect bites.

The man had lived alone, with only his dog for company, for years. With few friends, his life had become a routine of subway rides, minor office work, and lonely evenings spent sitting in front of a television set. I talked to him for awhile, after I had treated the superficial wounds on his dog. As gently as possible, I told him not to worry but to call me if he had any other problems.

Two days later he was back on the phone. "They" had gotten his dog and really damaged it. The man was afraid to venture into his yard to save the stricken animal. I asked him to try and to bring the dog in again.

The dog looked terrible. It had burn-like streaks all over its body, very peculiar lesions. Something—and I began to think it might be the man himself—had caused a number of irritated paths across the body. I said I'd have to keep the dog at the office for several days.

"They'll be hungry," he said. "They'll turn on me."

I must have sounded unconvinced.

"All right. I'll try to catch some of them and bring them in," he said.

He left. I started work on his pet.

An hour later, the phone rang again. The man was literally babbling. His backyard was full of "them." The trees, the shrubs, the ground—and they were beginning to invade his back porch. He had managed to capture some of them and was about to try and get some more.

"Don't leave your office," he said, just before hanging up. "I'll be in. They exist!"

For a moment I debated calling Bellevue. The man was obviously in a state of excitement and, judging from what he had done to the dog, might be dangerous.

I explained the situation to Bill, who agreed to stick around after office hours in case the situation got out of hand. We waited for the arrival of the Brooklyn creatures.

The man brought them in. Several jars full of soft, slimy, ugly refugees from a science-fiction writer's nightmare. I could not identify them. And I had to agree with the elderly man: living with a backyard full of them would send me up the wall too. The smallest of them measured five inches long.

I had Bill take them to an uptown laboratory for analysis. The next morning we got the report. The creatures were common eastern slugs. But they should be much, much smaller. In fact, they couldn't possibly grow this large, not in this climate.

After being assured that the specimens could not exist, I called the man in Brooklyn and tried to piece together the history of this phenomenon.

The man lived in a low area of Brooklyn where moisture tended to collect. He had been away on vacation for a month and the sprinkler system in his lawn had broken down, thoroughly flooding his property. The weather had been terribly hot, then was followed by torrential summer downpours. When he returned, the invasion of the slugs began.

Evidently the unusual environmental conditions had caused a mutation. I showed the specimens to several parasitologists, and they were astounded. Slugs do get that big in other parts of the world. But not in Brooklyn, or anywhere else in the northern United States. And, thrown out of kilter with nature, they had become carnivorous, not unlike some species known in Europe.

When the ideal jungle conditions changed, the slugs were unable to support their giant size, and they died off. But the experience had so shaken the man that he refused to live in the house. He moved to a hotel and put his property up for sale.

During the winter, I like to run at the 92nd Street YMHA before office hours. They have a good indoor track and on busy days it is often the only real exercise

I get. One morning I was feeling pretty good, did an extra couple of miles, then realized I was going to be late for work.

I showered quickly, and within fifteen minutes was headed down Lexington Avenue in the old Rolls. It was snowing lightly, but the traffic was moving along with few delays. I was rolling along at about thirty miles an hour and had a green light at the Eighty-fifth Street intersection.

Suddenly, an elderly man stepped out in front of my car and started to cross against the light. There was no way to stop in time to avoid a collision. I hit the brakes, yanked the steering wheel hard to the left, and ran up onto the sidewalk.

People scattered. Missing the man by a yard and a streetlamp by inches, I managed to steer the car back into the road. I double-parked the car across the intersection, got out, and walked back. The pedestrians who had jumped aside were calmly brushing snow off their clothes and continuing on their way.

I was stunned. No one had been injured at this busy intersection, and I hadn't even smashed up the car. The elderly man had returned to the sidewalk and was staring at the traffic light, scratching his head.

"Why did you do that?" I said.

"You know, I always have trouble these days," he said, slowly. "I keep forgetting whether it's the green or the red I have to walk on. My son told me I shouldn't leave the house alone, but I can take care of myself. If I could only remember those colors." He was absolutely unperturbed.

What could I say? I turned, waited for the light, then

walked back to my car and opened the door. Just as I was about to slide in behind the wheel, I felt a pressure on my back.

I turned around and found myself nose to nose with a young man, probably in his twenties, who was holding a switchblade knife.

"This is a stickup, mister," he said.

I have a gun permit and sometimes carry a .38 revolver in the car. But it was on the passenger side, under my coat, and there was no chance of reaching it before he could carve me up. I was drained physically from the hard run at the YMHA, thoroughly shaken by having just missed killing a half-dozen pedestrians, and, to boot, was late for surgery at the office.

Without thinking, I said, "You're just lucky that I'm in a rush. Now, get the hell away from me before I lose my temper." And I turned around, got in the car, closed the door and drove off.

Halfway down the block, it occurred to me that I had just done a foolish thing. But it had worked. And I could see him in my rearview mirror, still standing in the street with the knife in his hand and his mouth hanging open. Then he looked around, quickly closed the knife and stuffed it in his pocket, and scampered back to the sidewalk. Making a living, no matter what field you are in, seems to be getting tougher all the time.

Llamas are perhaps the gentlest-looking beasts of burden in the world. If treated with respect, they go about the job of hauling cargo throughout the Andes with what seems like a quiet dignity. But if mistreated or overworked, they share the camel's habit of showing their displeasure by accurate and long-ranging regurgitation.

I was backstage at the New York City Opera one evening to treat a lamed pony and noticed a little boy hanging around a llama that was appearing in one of their lavish productions. The child, son of another cast member, was bored waiting for his parent to get off work and started teasing the animal.

I finished with the pony, changed from an examination jacket into a suit coat, and went over to tell the boy —who must have been nine or ten years old—to restrict his hostility if he valued his health. The llama picked that moment to extract his revenge, and I happened to be in the line of fire.

A stream of half-digested food hit both of us. I am sure the boy learned a lesson and discarded some of his ideas about how animals should be approached. And I learned a lesson, too. No amount of cleaning can salvage a suit that has been so graced by a llama's revenge.

About a year later, one of the llamas on the Brook farm in New Jersey developed a limp. I thought it might be caused by some sort of back problem, but there was no way to tell without X-rays. So Len loaded it into a truck and dropped it off at the office.

It was a full-grown llama, and although quite gentle, was much too large to leave wandering around the office when we had finished with the X-rays. I led it out the front door to wait for the arrival of the truck. The llama just about filled our tiny courtyard. With his back to the window, his nose reached to the sidewalk.

He stood quietly, returning the gaze of startled pedestrians and motorists. It was shortly after two o'clock, the classic hour for people who have a liquid lunch to return to their jobs.

Two young men in vested suits, discussing interests vested in the advertising game, came walking down the street. They were listing just a bit, fortified, perhaps, for an afternoon conference. I was standing by the llama holding his harness, and saw them coming. They were too intent on their conversation, however, to see us. But just as they passed, the nearest one looked up, straight into the eyes of the llama.

He never broke stride and never looked back. They swayed by.

"Joe," I heard him say, "my wife is right. No more drinking at lunch. I don't even want to tell you what I just saw."

I have to euthanize animals as part of my job. Sometimes simply because no one wants them, sometimes because they are critically ill. It is not the sort of profession that leads to a romanticized outlook on life and death, but I am proud to be a member of it. It is well known that we are quietly eliminating a number of species of animals that will never leave their footprints in the archaeological strata characterizing the time of man on this planet. For many of them, our zoos have become a final refuge.

Even with this in mind, there are humane groups that are very much against zoos. Their goals are admirable, but sometimes unrealistic. And part of my job as a zoo veterinarian is trying to balance the pressure from these outside groups with the hard-line capabilities of a city budget.

We had a complaint from one society about the baboon cage at the Central Park Zoo. It didn't look natural enough to them, and the baboon clan—a frenetic crowd at best—seemed nervous. The quarters were perfectly adequate, but to apease the society, we had a jungle background painted on the walls, and everyone was happy. The baboons, of course, couldn't have cared less about what color the walls were.

The lion cage looks small, considering the size of the beast. And some people, seeing our old friend Raunchy sleeping a lot, will assume that he simply hasn't room to get up and run around in. But it is rare, even in the wilds, that you will see an adult male lion not sleeping. If he is adequately fed, the size of his domain will make little difference. Lions simply sleep a lot.

Unfortunately, zoo vets don't.